THE BEST OF
The Proverbs 31
HOMEMAKER

Encouragement and Ideas for Wives and Mothers

Edited by
Jeannie Marendt DeSena
From the newsletter
founded and published by
Jennifer McHugh

Proverbs 31 Homemaker Press
Charlotte, North Carolina

4/21/97

*Happy Birthday Sandy,
I hope this book will be as
much as an Encouragement to you,
in your new role, as it was for me!
Enjoy your reading.
        much love & prayers,
                Donna*

Copyright © 1996 by Proverbs 31 Homemaker Press.
Reproduction in whole or in part without written permission is prohibited, except by a reviewer, who may quote brief passages in a review. Our authors retain the rights to their work.

Proverbs 31 Homemaker Press
P.O. Box 17155
Charlotte, NC 28270
(704) 849-2270

Library of Congress Catalog Card Number: 95-92751
International Standard Book Number: 0-9649507-8-2

Unless otherwise noted, all Scripture quotations are taken from the *Holy Bible, New International Version®*. Copyright © 1973, 1978, 1984 by International Bible Society. Used by permission of Zondervan Publishing House. All rights reserved. Verses marked TLB are taken from *The Living Bible*, copyright © 1971. Used by permission of Tyndale House Publishers, Inc., Wheaton, Illinois 60189. All rights reserved.

Lego® is a registered trademark of Interlego, A.G.
SpaghettiOs® is a registered trademark of Campbell Soup Company.

Edited, designed, and typeset by Jeannie Marendt DeSena
Proverbs 31 Homemaker logo designed by Sharen Swintek

Manufactured in the United States of America

10 9 8 7 6 5 4 3 2

Dedication

For my parents, Judy and Dick Marendt,
who raised me with a strong faith;
for my husband, Curtis,
whose love and faith in me never falter;
and for my daughter, Olivia,
who has re-opened my eyes to the wonder of God's world.
— J.M.D.

Dedicated to my loving husband, Mike,
who has surpassed all of my expectations in a husband.
Thanks for keeping me going these last three years
with the Proverbs 31 Ministry. Without your
ever-constant support, there would be no ministry.
I love you!
— J.M.

Contents

6	Proverbs 31:10-31
8	From the Editor / *Jeannie Marendt DeSena*

CHILDREN OF GOD
11	My Life, God's Garment / *Debra Yeatts*
12	Reasons to Endure / *Kevin Woody*
14	A Homemaker's Prayer / *Shirley Gray*
15	When Do You Pray? / *Jennifer McHugh*
16	Quiet-Time Testimonies / *Marybeth Whalen, Christine Anderson, Ruth Ann Wilson, Susan Godley*
18	Alive in the Lord / *Jennifer McHugh*
19	Pray About WHAT?? / *Jennifer McHugh*
20	Children of God / *Debra Yeatts*

THE MAN I LOVE
21	Helpmates Wanted / *Jennifer McHugh*
23	Husband-napped! / *Jennifer McHugh*
24	The Traveling Man / *Meg Avey*
25	A Poem for My Husband / *Carol Mader*
26	The Hardest Part of Marriage / *Meredith Banks*
28	He Won't Go to Church / *Kevin Woody*
30	A Question in Her Eyes / *Kevin Woody*

THE GOOD, THE BAD, & THE MESSY
33	Mothers Matter / *Carol L. Baldwin*
35	A Father's Treasure / *Kevin Woody*
36	What Should I Do? / *Marybeth Whalen*
38	Train Up A Child / *Susan Gardner*
40	Respecting the Individual / *Nancee Skipper*
42	The Perfect Day / *Jeannie Marendt DeSena*
44	The Supermom Syndrome / *Jennifer McHugh*
45	Homemaker Blues / *Janet Steddum*
46	The Overscheduled Family / *Meg Avey*
47	Punishment or Discipline? / *Michelle Woody*
49	Accidents Happen / *Meg Avey*
51	Building a Household / *Shirley Gray*
52	SpaghettiO® Stains / *Kevin Woody*
53	Makin' Memories / *Nancee Skipper*

WORDS FROM THE WISE

- 55 We Need Naomis! / *Jennifer McHugh*
- 56 From the "Mentee" / *Jennifer McHugh*
- 58 From the Mentor / *Ruth Ann Wilson*
- 59 That First Grandchild / *Sue Rudolph*
- 60 I Saw You Today / *Anonymous*
- 62 Helping Each Other / *Cheryl Bessett*
- 64 The Value of Friendship / *Marybeth Whalen*
- 65 Donna Otto: Mentors for Moms / *Marybeth Whalen*
- 67 Wild, Wonderful Becky Tirabassi / *Jennifer McHugh*
- 68 A Conversation with Marilyn Quayle / *Lysa TerKeurst*
- 71 Making Time for Yourself / *Nancee Skipper*

OF PURSE STRINGS & APRON STRINGS

- 73 My Hunk of Burning Love / *Lysa TerKeurst*
- 75 It's Not in the Budget / *Janet Steddum*
- 76 I Won't Make My Own Soap! / *Brent Wainscott*
- 78 Food for Thought / *Janet Steddum*
- 80 Winning the Grocery Game / *Janet Steddum*
- 81 Eating Out for Less / *Janet Steddum*
- 82 Down-to-Earth Decorating / *Rhonda Jaynes, Meredith Banks, Marybeth Whalen*

HOLIDAYS & EVERYDAYS

- 85 Every Day is Valentine's Day / *Meg Avey*
- 87 Making Birthdays Special / *Jennifer McHugh*
- 88 Is It Just the Thought that Counts? / *Marybeth Whalen*
- 89 Hatching the Easter Story / *Susan Yount and Sidney Dunlap*
- 91 Harried Holidays / *Jennifer McHugh*
- 93 A New Year's Tradition / *Beth McKnight*
- 93 A Year's Worth of Ideas: The Proverbs 31 Homemaker Activity Calendar

- 106 Recommended Reading
- 108 About our Authors
- 111 About the Ministry

PROVERBS 31: 10-31

A WIFE OF NOBLE CHARACTER who can find? She is worth far more than rubies. Her husband has full confidence in her and lacks nothing of value. She brings him good, not harm, all the days of her life. She selects wool and flax and works with eager hands. She is like the merchant ships, bringing her food from afar. She gets up while it is still dark; she provides food for her family and portions for her servant girls.

She considers a field and buys it; out of her earnings she plants a vineyard. She sets about her work vigorously; her arms are strong for her tasks. She sees that her trading is profitable, and her lamp does not go out at night. In her hand she holds the distaff and grasps the spindle with her fingers.

She opens her arms to the poor and extends her hands to the needy. When it snows, she has no fear for her household; for all of them are clothed in scarlet. She makes coverings for her bed; she is clothed in fine linen and purple. Her husband is respected at the city gate, where he takes his seat among the elders of the land. She makes linen garments and sells them, and supplies the merchants with sashes. She is clothed with strength and dignity; she can laugh at the days to come.

    She speaks with wisdom, and faithful instruction is on her tongue. She watches over the affairs of her household and does not eat the bread of idleness. Her children arise and call her blessed; her husband also, and he praises her: "Many women do noble things, but you surpass them all."

CHARM IS DECEPTIVE, and beauty is fleeting; but a woman who fears the Lord is to be praised. Give her the reward she has earned, and let her works bring her praise at the city gate.

From the Editor

IN FEBRUARY OF 1992, A lonely homemaker struggled with her roles of wife and new mother in an unfamiliar city. Her neighborhood seemed like a ghost town each weekday after men and women took their children to school and child-care and trooped off to work. Long, diaper-filled days stretched before her. Surely there must be other Christian women at home like me, she thought — so she started a monthly newsletter to find and encourage them.

Since Jennifer McHugh mailed out 30 copies of her first issue to supportive friends and family members in August 1992, *The Proverbs 31 Homemaker* has grown into a multi-faceted ministry, with a newsletter readership of more than 2,000 throughout the United States and three countries, one-day conferences around the nation, and encouragement groups that offer women support and friendship. The word has spread through a nationwide radio ministry; articles in such prominent newspapers as *The Charlotte Observer*, *Philadelphia Inquirer*, and *Arizona Republic*; and television appearances on "The Sally Jessy Raphael Show," "The 700 Club," and a BBC television newsmagazine in England.

Where Jennifer and husband Mike once spent days folding, labeling, and stamping each issue of the newsletter themselves, now a cluster of volunteers crowds into the McHughs' living room one Tuesday evening a month — managing to prepare more than 1,000 copies for mailing in between prayer and fellowship. Jennifer was joined in the summer of 1994 by a partner with a flair for marketing, Lysa TerKeurst, who is the voice of the radio ministry and the force behind its growth from one local market to more than 80 stations across the country. And as the ministry has expanded, other dedicated women have contributed time and ideas. During the life of the newsletter, readers have kept up with the growth in the McHugh family as well; the baby Jennifer wrote about in the early issues, their precious daughter Morgan, has become a big sister to Mary Madison and Jake.

Volunteers swap stories about what they expected the first time they met Jennifer and visited her home. "I thought she'd be in a business suit and pearls." "I expected June Cleaver to greet me at the door with a plate of cookies." "I thought she and the girls would be wearing Laura Ashley mother-daughter jumpers and matching hairbows." The details vary with each description, but the common thread is there: We figured someone else had it all together the way we wished we did. "When you met the 'real Jennifer,' were you disappointed or relieved?" I asked. They answered in chorus: "Relieved!" We learned as we got to know her

From the Editor

that, while she has energy and determination that don't quit and faith in the Lord to match, she faces some of the same problems the rest of us do. Her house isn't always spotless. Her husband travels a lot. She hates to cook. Her kids have had some serious illnesses. She tends to overcommit herself. And her dog can be, shall we say, *embarrassingly* friendly. Readers of the newsletter know these things; Jennifer shares her struggles and triumphs as a Christian homemaker in each issue.

In the short time I have been associated with the Proverbs 31 Homemaker Ministry as a newsletter subscriber, volunteer, and now book editor, Jennifer, Lysa, and other "real people" have inspired me to be a better Christian woman, wife, and mother. I appreciate the homemaking tips and other how-to's I read, but mostly I am soaking up the example of Christians who have their priorities in order and live accordingly. These contributors are not portraying themselves as models of motherhood (or fatherhood, for some of the writers are men) and saintliness.

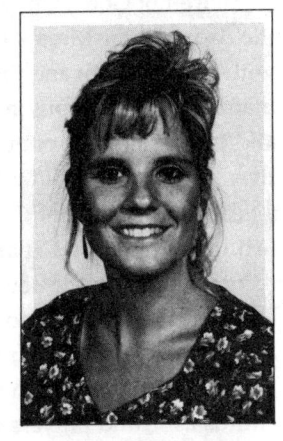

Jennifer McHugh

They don't claim to have all the answers. But as Ruth Ann Wilson writes in "From the Mentor," they know the One who does. Even more important to me than the practical things I've learned — such as the titles of some good devotional literature for my toddler, ways to meet and encourage other homemakers, and fun ideas from the monthly activity calendar — are the spiritual truths contained in the newsletter's first-person essays and features: It is not just the person whose life is free of problems who must praise God. We serve Christ as we serve our families. Give each day to the Lord with thanks.

That was my perspective when Jennifer approached me and said, "We want to do a book, the best of the first three years of *The Proverbs 31 Homemaker*." She put all 36 issues of the newsletter in my hands and a great deal of trust in my judgment. I wanted the book to serve as an introduction to the ministry for readers unfamiliar with the newsletter, a new look at a cherished friend for longtime subscribers, and a compendium of helpful, uplifting writing of the sort not found in the secular press. Like any homemaker, I had to live within my budget, so it was impossible to include every one of the many articles that touched me. As clear themes emerged, each selection had to strengthen its chapter and the book as a whole as well as stand out individually.

Jennifer writes frequently of ordering her life with God first, husband second, and children third; the book unfolds in the same way. A chapter apiece is devoted to these three most important relationships in a homemaker's life (Chapter One, "Children of God"; Chapter Two, "The Man I Love"; Chapter Three, "The Good, the Bad, and the Messy"). The book also addresses the homemaker's need for time with other women and time for herself (Chapter Four, "Words from the Wise"), the management of a household (Chapter Five, "Of Purse Strings and Apron Strings"), and the importance of making every day special (Chapter Six, "Holidays and Everydays"). In addition to essays, *The Best of The Proverbs 31 Homemaker* also offers a year-long version of the activity calendar, one of the newsletter's most popular features. Also included are a reading list, which categorizes books that have been recommended in the newsletter, and biographical sketches for contributors who, by the time you read and re-read their words, will feel like friends.

Friends are important to the Proverbs 31 Homemaker Ministry. Like this book, the ministry began as an idea, and it has been nurtured by the hard work, enthusiasm, and prayers of many people. While there isn't room enough to list everyone, these are some of the people who have helped the Lord, Jennifer, and Lysa make the ministry what it is today: the staff at WRCM, 91.9 FM in Charlotte, the ministry's "flagship" radio station; Chick-fil-A at the Arboretum in Charlotte; conference coordinator Beth Russell; encouragement group coordinator Jennifer Schroeder; encouragement group leaders Molly Dragstrem, Molly Faulkner, Jacque Garner, and Sandra Holland; tireless volunteers Lynn Black, Julie Dietz, Brookes Eiler, Monica Everhardt, Stacey Holcombe, Marie Kovitch, Katrina Kuitems, Molly McHugh, Donna Rich, Sue Rudolph, Renee Swope, Stephanie Turek, Martha Wilson, and Mindy Winters; and past staff members Nancy Absher, who entered all 1,000-plus subscribers into a new database and performed countless other administrative tasks, and Marybeth Whalen, who ably edited the newsletter for a year and coordinated the first Proverbs 31 Conference. And we cannot overlook the newsletter's faithful readers and contributors. Many, many thanks to each and every one.

To the ministry's acknowledgments, I add my own. Thank you: Marybeth Whalen, for suggesting me for this project; Jennifer McHugh and Lysa TerKeurst, for taking that suggestion; Jill Bond, Kathy Chiero, Dr. Norm Geisler, and Donna Otto, for reviewing the manuscript; Shane Wolf, of Ship to Shore Inc., for your valuable pointers; and Curtis, my husband, for the myriad ways you have shown your support during this project. May the book glorify God and help my neighbor.

— *Jeannie Marendt DeSena*

CHAPTER ONE

CHILDREN OF GOD

Jesus called out in a loud voice, "Father, into your hands I commit my spirit" (Luke 23:46).

My Life, God's Garment
by Debra Yeatts

HAVE YOU EVER CONSIDERED your life a garment made by God? When He chose me He had a pattern, and I was like fabric that needed to be cut out and pieced together.

The beginning steps come together quickly, with straight seams and few details. A snitch of time here and there pulls the pieces together, and the garment takes shape. A new creation, a new Christian, a new dress.

Suddenly, it becomes obvious that the fabric has taken form. I can tell what it is to become, and others can see it, too. Without explanation, I begin to witness God's hand at work in my life.

Then comes the detail work. Basting threads need to be pulled out, one by one. Painstakingly, He searches me for hidden strings of self-reliance, self-destruction, shame, bitterness, false humility, guilt, fear, and selfishness. Each seam and gather is a hiding place for sin. I begin to feel His personal involvement in my life as He purifies, quickens, and calls me to Him.

Every detail is important. Each step distinguishes a quality dress from one that is left unfinished. The pattern's Creator knows that the next step involves sewing on His promises that will hold me together... buttons of faith, snaps of hope, and hooks of love. Promises that He will never fail me and will always provide for me.

Sewing can be frustrating and tedious at times. The pattern can be confusing and complicated to the one who isn't the designer. But to the Creator, it is the perfect process to the transformed life.

Such is my life in the Master's hand, as God works with me through the power of the Holy Spirit. Like a garment in the making, my surrender to His will is another stitch toward dependence on Him. He molds me, pulls me, and teaches me perseverance in the trials of life. My trials provide an opportunity to know God better, and knowing God is the secret to a full and blessed life.

Father, I too commit my spirit to you for your handiwork.

❖

Reasons to Endure
by Kevin Woody

DAN AND DAVE. YOU REMEMBER the two handsome athletes in commercials promoting Reebok shoes prior to the 1992 Summer Olympic Games. A small problem developed; Dan O'Brien did not make the U.S. team. His failure was highly publicized throughout the sporting and advertising worlds. He could have withdrawn and hidden in his sorrow. Instead, he chose to endure. One month after watching the Olympic Games, he broke the world record in the decathlon with a score of 8,891 points. Endurance has its rewards.

What are the overwhelming failures, obstacles, and challenges in your life right now? Endurance may be the key to success. "Oh, boy!" I'm sure you are saying. I agree, endurance rarely is an exciting process. For many of you, endurance involves the daily routine of raising your children in a world where few adults see or reward your faithful efforts. Why should we keep trying?

In Philippians 3:12, Paul writes, "...but I press on to take hold of that for which Christ Jesus took hold of me. Friends, I do not consider myself yet to have taken hold of it. But one thing I do: Forgetting what is behind and

> *In those circumstances that require long-term obedience, be assured that God always rewards faithfulness.*

straining toward what is ahead, I press on toward the goal to win the prize for which God has called me heavenward in Christ Jesus."

In this inspiring message, we find three reasons to endure. First, endurance results in reward. In those circumstances that require long-term obedience, be assured that God *always* rewards faithfulness. In 1 Corinthians 9:24-25, Paul exhorts, "Run in such a way as to get the prize... a crown that will last forever." Work through the drudgery of routines, the fits of preschoolers, and the brokenness of an important relationship — such action will bring reward. No one else may know of your efforts and commitment, but God sees every detail. The prize may be distant, but it will not be delayed from His perfect timing for delivery.

Second, endurance is a way by which God shapes us. If clay could speak, it would probably say to the potter, "Get your hands off me. I'm happy being a blob!" In the midst of our great struggles, we ask God, "What are you trying to do to me? I can't take any more." Because we are in the middle, it is difficult to perceive that God is shaping us into something far more beautiful than we are now. Through endurance, we submit to God's effort to make us more like Christ. As Paul said, not yet have we "been made perfect" (Philippians 3:12). Note that Paul used the passive voice; he knew that God was working on him.

Have you ever seen a tigress take hold of one of her cubs? She simply picks up the energetic babe in her powerful jaws and moves her offspring wherever she wants. It is a picture of absolute dominance. In the same way, the maturing disciple submits to the dominance of Christ, "taking hold of that for which Christ Jesus took hold of me." The third reason to endure is that by so doing, we acknowledge that Christ possesses us. Choosing to endure in difficulties says to the world, "I trust God to do whatever is necessary for the completion of His plans."

Endurance is challenging. It is painful. It is expensive. But it is always worth the effort.

❖

A Homemaker's Prayer
by Shirley Gray

*L*ORD, HELP ME TO NOT *become weary in my well doing. Help me to see that everything I do in my home is important, and to do it for Your glory. I want to keep my eyes on heavenly rewards and not just the day-to-day tasks. Help me to look to You for encouragement in my daily routine. I want to make You foremost in my home.* **Amen.**

When Do You Pray?
by Jennifer McHugh

I CAN THINK OF MANY times when I set my alarm to get up early in order to spend some time alone with my Heavenly Father. Despite my good intentions, either I overslept or my children beat the alarm clock. I would rush into the day and feel guilty for not spending time with Jesus. This is a common problem, especially for those of us with small children. What should we do? Not have a quiet time? Put the kids off until the quiet time is over?

I don't think the Lord would want us to put our kids off while we spend time with Him. It seems to me that they would grow to resent our time with the Lord when we should be teaching them how wonderful that time is. I do believe, though, that after their needs (like breakfast) have been met, there is nothing wrong with teaching them that Mommy has some time to talk to Jesus and pray for her family every day. I think we sometimes feel our children should be entertained every moment of every day. By allowing them to entertain themselves, they learn self-discipline.

If finding time in the morning sounds impossible to you, try having your quiet time at lunch. Christian author and speaker Becky Tirabassi, a wonderful role model for all of us, suggests that we "make an appointment with the King every day." She says to write it in your day planner and to have a back-up plan in case the first appointment goes awry. In other words, if your morning goes crazy, plan on spending a quiet hour with the Lord at nap time. Children are never too old to have a quiet hour, even if they have outgrown their nap. If they are older, encourage them to spend some time talking to Jesus.

Another way to include the children in your worship is to allot them a page in your prayer journal. Each day, pray together for whatever is on that page and rejoice with them when God answers prayers. They will learn that you go to God for your needs and that they can, too. Play worshipful music or children's Christian tunes. Listening to music is a great way to learn Scripture and focus on Christ.

If you miss a quiet time, don't allow Satan to hold that over your head. Remember that "tomorrow is another day." We should be in prayer and communion with the Lord throughout the day, anyway, not just during a set time.

God has given us our precious children and understands better than anyone the demands that are placed on us. Know that He is patient and kind and loving and is always available for you, even during your 2 a.m. feeding!

❖

Be still, and know that I am God... (Psalm 46:10).

Quiet-Time Testimonies

• Find quiet time at baby's nap time

Since I have a baby who is often up at dawn, I find it difficult to get up before her. However, I almost always have at least one hour of peace in the afternoon when both of my children are asleep. This is truly "quiet time" for me. These few minutes leave me refreshed and ready for the hectic dinner hour and for my husband's arrival home from work.

— Marybeth Whalen

• Sing a song unto the Lord

I find spiritual music to be a good way to have fellowship with the Holy Spirit. I have four children and have not always had a block of time to dedicate to studying God's word. However, I can listen to a sweet, reverent song while washing dishes or spending time with my children and feel the Holy Spirit working in my life.

Another way I have my quiet time is through a family Bible study with my husband and children. Ideally, I have my own personal quiet time *and* the time with my family, but that's not always possible.

Another tip I can share is that I always pray before my quiet time and ask the Lord to reveal to me what He would have me know. It really sets a reverent tone for studying God's word.

— *Christine Anderson*

• Pray throughout the day

I know how difficult it can be to find time alone with the Lord. If you will ask Him to show you when you can find time in your day for communion with Him, He will answer.

There is no place where we are told our devotional time has to be. I have devotions in the bathroom, in the bedroom, in the kitchen while cooking, in the car, and in parking lots while waiting for kids to finish lessons or appointments.

When we had small babies and I was getting up in the night, I would use that time to pray. It was a special time that I missed when the children grew older and were weaned.

— *Ruth Ann Wilson*

• Get an early start

Like most mothers of small children, I found it difficult to set aside precious moments each day for a quiet time. The Lord has promised to honor those who honor Him, so when I committed myself to rising before dawn each morning for quiet time, I knew the Lord would give me the strength and energy I needed to keep up with my two young sons.

I have found that now my days are more focused and peaceful when I start each one in the presence of the Lord.

— *Susan Godley*

Alive in the Lord
by Jennifer McHugh

*I*T'S EASY TO GET INTO the "same-old, same-old" in our quiet times. Here are a few suggestions for keeping your relationship with the Lord alive and going!

1. **Find a prayer partner.** Make a commitment to pray for her daily. Once a week, call her and see how God is working in her life. Take a few minutes to pray together over the phone.

2. **Read a book** (fiction or non-fiction) about a person who served God. This always gets me excited about my life with the Lord.

> *Reading a book about a person who served God always gets me excited about my life with the Lord.*

3. **Write a prayer** for your children. Write it neatly, do it in needlepoint, or cross-stitch it, and give it to them on a special day.

4. **Plan a date with God.** Make a special date to get away for an entire day by yourself to really spend some quality time with your Lord.

5. Get away for a night with another couple or a friend. **Spend the evening in fellowship** specifically sharing your needs and prayers. Together, lay them before the Lord. I know two couples who do this each year. They pray for their children and situations in their lives. What a wonderful way to fellowship!

6. **Start a prayer journal.** Record your prayers to see God's hand in your life, and praise God for His answers!

7. **Make every Friday your Praise Day.** Spend your prayer time thanking and praising God.

Pray about WHAT??
by Jennifer McHugh

ARE YOU GUILTY OF TELLING someone you will pray about something and then forgetting that promise by prayer time? You're not alone.

Organizing my prayer life was difficult. I wanted to pray for people, but I could never remember everything. Finally I figured out that I never would remember unless I kept some type of record. I do not like to write, so a journal is something I knew I would never maintain.

After considering the possibilities, I decided on note cards. I keep my cards in a box with a rubber band around them. Each note card has one name at the top. On the left-hand side of the card is the date that I began praying for that request. After the prayer is answered, I highlight it.

After some time, I had so many cards that I was having difficulty praying for everything every day, so I divided the cards into days of the week. For instance, on Mondays I pray for my friends who do not know Jesus Christ as their Savior. On Tuesdays, I pray for friends in the ministry (in missions, as pastors, etc.). I also have a stack of cards I refer to daily — for family and friends I have committed to praying for on a regular basis.

This system has worked well for me. The most exciting part is that I can look back and see how God has worked in people's lives! The system is concise and does not require a lot of writing. I have maintained my prayer cards for two years now (longer than I have maintained any other kind of organization).

You can add a picture to your card if it will help you to pray. I have a picture of a couple my husband and I have never met, whom we support financially. This visual aid helps me to focus on them and their needs.

You can set up your own system for quiet time. This note-card system is a way for me to remember to pray about things that I would otherwise forget.

Our Father who art in heaven, hallowed be thy name (Matthew 6:9).

Children of God
by Debra Yeatts

WHAT DOES IT REALLY MEAN to call God, the Lord of the universe, our Father? Do we truly know God as a gracious loving parent? To be or to act as a parent has new meaning for me now that I'm one to my children.

Who are we in Christ? "To all who have received Him, to those who believe in His name, He granted the right to become children of God" (John 1:12). And that is what we are! See how much our heavenly Father loves us, for He allows us to be called His children (1 John 3:1). God chose us, and He has made us heirs with a great inheritance.

It's so easy to forget who we are and that we can go to God to ask Him to do something special for us. As a mother at home with preschoolers, I need to feel loved. I also need strength, stability, and companionship. Often I feel that I need my mother to come live with us! Prayerfully, I asked God to show me His attributes. He answers my prayer by showing me that as I am parenting my children, He is parenting me.

Daily I ponder the comparison of my children depending on me as I depend on God. As my children come to me with their many needs, I picture myself as a child going to God with the same requests. His hands serve better than mine, His heart is pure, and His ways of discipline are perfect. He will carry me all the days of my life just as a man carries his child (Deuteronomy 1:31). He is love (John 3:16). He is rich in mercy (Ephesians 2:4). He loves me with the same intensity with which He loves His son, Jesus (John 17:23). Is that really possible? He will not let anything separate me from His love (Romans 8:35-39). He revives me when I'm exhausted (Isaiah 40:28-31)!

What do we know about God's character? He reveals Himself as we pray, so our challenge is to make prayer a daily habit. Pray as you know how, and trust God to reveal more of Himself to you.

Oh Father, help us to know that we are precious in your sight. Assure us of your love and remind us that you are absolutely trustworthy. May you rejoice over us with singing.

CHAPTER TWO

THE MAN I LOVE

"... a man will leave his father and mother and be united to his wife, and the two will become one flesh" (Mark 10: 7-8).

Helpmates Wanted
by Jennifer McHugh

MARRIAGE IS SUCH AN IMPORTANT gift God has given us. We often get so caught up in our children, which is easy to do because we are spending our days with them. Our lives become so involved with theirs. We take care of their physical needs, and we pray over and contemplate often their emotional, spiritual, and social needs. When our beloved husbands come home, we want to share everything our children are doing with them.

We were designed first to be a helpmate to our husbands. God created us because it wasn't good for man to be alone. In these days of self-fulfillment and total independence, this message is like salt in a wound. We don't like hearing it, but it is a beautiful and wonderful gift from our Lord.

Go back and search the Scriptures on what the role of a wife is. Look at Proverbs 31 and see what role this wife took. We are not to lose our identities and become doormats to our spouses, we are to complete them. God put you with your husband for a special purpose. Together you complete a pattern.

I know that our husbands are imperfect, but so are we. Pray daily for your husband, and ask God to give you an attitude of love for him. Remember that your first job in the home is to serve God. Your second is to love and respect your husband, and your third duty is to your children.

Try these suggestions from different wives on how to love your husband:

- Hide notes around the house telling him you love him and are glad you married him.
- Swap out children with another family so you and your mate can have one weekend a month alone together. We spend so much time sacrificing for our children. Go the extra mile to do the same for your husband. If you can't afford to get away, spend the weekend alone at home together.
- Have a surprise party for your husband when he gets home from work. Hang a banner and balloons, and have the kids draw pictures. Fix his favorite meal. At dinner, have everyone at the table share what they love about Daddy. Don't wait until a special occasion to do this.
- Play games together one night. Turn off the television and pull out the board games or cards.
- Give him a bath, wash his hair, and then blow dry it.
- Try not to talk on the phone a lot when he is home.
- Meet him at the door with soft music playing, the phone off the hook, and the children at a neighbor's or friend's house one afternoon. Dress appropriately.

Remember that your husband was hand-picked by God for you. In a world where we are so focused on our own needs, wants, and desires, it is much more difficult to love that imperfect, human man you married.

Thank you, Lord, for my husband. Help me to remember to love him.

Husband-napped!
by Jennifer McHugh

I CAN'T KEEP A SECRET from Mike, my husband. If I even try to plan something, he knows it. But I finally pulled it off, and thought I'd share the story with you.

My husband was extremely stressed out at his new job and needed a break. I decided to get away with him for the weekend. I called his boss and asked her to schedule an afternoon meeting with Mike.

I asked a friend to keep my little girl for a couple of days (which I repaid when she and her husband went to Australia!) and picked Mike up for lunch. Believe it or not, I kept a straight face until we hit the interstate and he asked exactly where we were going for lunch.

He looked in the back of the van at our packed suitcases and said, "I'm not going back to work, am I?" After I assured him that his boss was in on the plan, he took his tie off and kicked back to relax.

We stopped in a little town outside of Charlotte for a picnic lunch and drove on to the mountains. What a wonderful getaway!

I strongly recommend it for you. If you're like me and have a tough time keeping a secret, make plans as late as possible. That way you don't have to keep a straight face for long. Happy planning!

When was the last time:

- You told your husband what a wonderful provider he is?
- You dressed up in a nightie for him?
- You went to a marriage conference together?
- You went out on a date?
- You wrote your husband a love letter?

Remember to take time to make your husband feel special! He's worth it!

The Traveling Man
by Meg Avey

HERE IS A QUESTION ALL of you travel widows can answer: When does a major appliance break down? Right! As soon as your husband leaves for a trip! There are several ways of handling this unhappy situation; one (which I still use occasionally) is to sit down and cry! However, the good Lord in all His wisdom and timing put this rough spot there for a reason. Someday we will know why, but in the meantime we have to deal with it.

I've experienced everything from sickness to Hurricane Hugo without the support of my husband. One time my husband was gone for three weeks to Korea and Singapore. While he was away I was very busy. In the span of three days I "bagged a Jag" (rear-ended a Jaguar) and received a ticket for going over

> *I have learned to lean on Jesus and His word for strength when my husband is away on business trips.*

the posted speed. You don't want to imagine the wonderful telephone conversation my husband and I shared that week!

I believe the Lord allows these things to happen to strengthen us. Often I find myself leaning too much on my husband instead of doing for myself. I have learned to lean on Jesus and His word for strength when my husband is gone. Psalm 46:1 says, "God is our refuge and strength, an ever-present help in trouble." Trouble could mean that broken dishwasher, a sick child up all night, car problems, or anything that requires extra attention. Turn to God for your strength, and then tackle the problem yourself. Perhaps God just wants you to know what wonderful talents you possess.

A Poem for My Husband
by Carol Mader

WHILE YOU WORK, you give us the most cherished of all
treasures
TIME
time...
for snuggling and cuddling
two morning-tousled lifeforms
beneath magical tents of sheets

Time...
to throw away the shopping plans
because it's ugly outside
and there's always tomorrow
Now we have time...
for glitter messes
and chocolate batter kisses

Time
to explore puddles
mountains of books
and the depths of our imagination
Your efforts allow me time...
to shape and mold
and rock and hold

Thank You for time to teach the truth about God
Thank you for adhering to unyielding, grinding schedules
so that we can dance to the flow of the music each day
Thank you, my husband
for fighting traffic, office politics and the sterile
business world
to give us...

Time
Together
Your sphere of equations and meetings opens our world
to a deeper understanding of one another
Thank you for staring into a computer screen every day
So that I can gaze into
our children's big, hungry eyes all day long
Thank you from all of us
We know how lucky we are.

❖

The Hardest Part of Marriage
by Meredith Banks

RECENTLY I HAD A CONVERSATION with a longtime friend who is engaged to be married. She was asking me some questions about what it is like being a wife. Although we grew up together and have very similar backgrounds, there is a difference between us. I have invited Jesus Christ into my heart and committed my life to Him.

As she continued to question me, I tried to answer her as openly and honestly as possible so I could offer her advice and also share my faith with her. Things were sailing along smoothly when she asked me *the* question: "What do you think is the hardest part about being a wife?" For me, this one was easy, because I have struggled with one particular thing for what seems like eternity.

I looked her straight in the eye and told her, "The hardest part about being a wife is being submissive to my husband."

"WHAT?!" she shrieked. "Being submissive! What are you talking about? This is the '90s — all of that 'obey' stuff is ancient history. Do you actually believe that you must obey your husband?"

As the words tumbled out of her mouth, it was clear to me how differently the world views the role of the wife from the way God views that role.

I gently tried to explain this to her, and I opened my Bible and showed her Ephesians 5:22-24. It says, "Wives, submit to your husbands as to the Lord. For

> *"WHAT?!" she shrieked. "Being submissive! This is the '90s — all of that 'obey' stuff is ancient history."*

the husband is the head of the wife as Christ is the head of the church, His body, of which He is the Savior. Now as the church submits to Christ, so also wives should submit to their husbands in everything."

There it was in black and white, clearly stated and easily understood. Yet she continued on, "People don't actually believe that anymore, though. Not to mention, I know several religious women who don't believe in that submission garbage."

What she said was true; there are many "religious" people who no longer believe in submission on the part of the wife. The Bible calls this being conformed to this world.

As our conversation continued, my friend was still shocked, to say the least. I can't say that I blame her. In today's world of car phones, computers, and career women, it is easy to become desensitized to God's word. We must remember that although being submissive is very difficult at times, this is God's will for us, and He will always give us the grace and strength we need to prevail.

My friend told me she thought there was no way that she could ever be submissive to a man. The way I view submission is not to a man but to God, obeying Him and His word. The way God planned marriage is for the wife to put the Lord first, her husband second, and herself next. The husband is to put the Lord first, then his wife, and finally himself. If we follow God's guidelines, our marriages will be strong, and our love for one another will overflow because we are in unison with God's plan for us.

Take a look at your life and your marriage. Are you being the wife God designed you to be? He has given us clear instructions and examples such as the woman in Proverbs 31. Here is what to do:

- Pray that God will show you how to be a godly wife.
- Read Proverbs 31 and Ephesians 5 daily.
- Pray that you will be sensitive to the Holy Spirit's teaching.
- Put your trust in God and allow Him to work out His will in your life.

Then stand back and embrace the new you, and experience the love, joy, and contentment that can only come from God.

❖

He Won't Go to Church
by Kevin Woody

"WHY WON'T MY HUSBAND GO to church?" "Why does he always expect me to lead in family prayers and Bible reading?" "How can I help him to know God or grow mature in his relationship with Jesus?" These are common questions of Christian wives today. Every Sunday, church meetings draw a large number of wives whose husbands "already had a commitment today."

What can a woman do to encourage her husband to love and serve the Lord? The most common effort is to get him to church. Gently and kindly, a wife may ask her husband to attend worship this Sunday with the rest of the family. He may come or he may not, but often no great difference in his life develops. The pattern of a wife's invitation and a husband's refusal can become a painful problem in the life of a family. The longer the process continues, the more deeply resistant to church a husband becomes. Often the encouragement to attend church becomes counterproductive.

The apostle Peter recognized this same problem in the early churches. God inspired him to write guidelines for the wife longing to see her husband in Christ:

Wives, in the same way be submissive to your husbands so that, if any of them do not believe the word, they may be won over without words by the behavior of their

---

The challenge for the wife of the unbelieving or spiritually lazy husband is to make her life and actions stunningly beautiful, as much like Christ's as possible.

---

wives, when they see the purity and reverence of your lives. Your beauty should not come from outward adornment.... Instead, it should be that of your inner self, the unfading beauty of a gentle and quiet spirit... (I Peter 3:1-4).

I think every church needs a W.O.W.W., or "won over without words," group — women encouraging each other in their ministry to their husbands. The challenge for the wife of the unbelieving or spiritually lazy husband is to make her life and actions stunningly beautiful. Her life becomes so much like Christ's, so full of grace, power, gentleness, and service, that her husband wants to know more.

You know from experience that you can't control your husband. You have influence, but not control. What Peter challenges the wife to focus on is what she *can* control — her own obedience to Christ.

Keep in mind that it is the wife's job to demonstrate the gospel and her love for Christ by her behavior. The Holy Spirit, and He alone, has the ability to convict individuals of their sin and their need for Christ.

Leading a husband to Christ is hard work. Sometimes it is a long process. Give him the room he needs to think, question, and discover, and commit yourself to making your life so beautiful that he will want to know who dressed you.

❖

A Question in Her Eyes
by Kevin Woody

RECENTLY I WENT TO VISIT a friend at the hospital. Vivian was laying uncomfortably in her bed after major back surgery. As I held her soft, tender hand and looked into her eyes, time stopped. I had never before seen Vivian without her glasses. I peered deeply into the beauty of her crystal blue eyes. Funny thing, but one aspect that doesn't seem to fade, wrinkle, or change with age is the color of our eyes. I am 29 years old; Vivian is 71. She and Grady have been married for more than fifty years.

The Lord questioned me as I gazed into Vivian's eyes. He said, "Your wife, whose eyes are so blue, will someday age as this woman has. How will you love her then?"

As Mother's Day approached, I considered that question. How will I love her then? How have I loved her in our past? How do I love her today?

Motherhood has brought great changes to our family. The most obvious ones are different time patterns, more responsibility, and the tension of learning to share my wife with someone cuter than I am. I appreciate what motherhood has done to my wife. Because of our children, she has grown more contemplative and mature. I am attracted more to her because of her growing leadership abilities. Daily she leads a band of three little soldiers who have yet to grasp the teachings of life's basic training — or potty training, for that matter.

I am drawn to her feminine strength, a strength unique from that of men. I see it in her long hours of cleaning, washing, feeding, and playing. Every day

> *I appreciate what motherhood has done to my wife. Because of our children, she has grown more contemplative and mature. I am drawn to her feminine strength.*

she goes through these demanding efforts knowing that tomorrow our children will need the same acts of love all over again. I lack that kind of strength.

Her body has changed. Pregnancy does leave its lasting marks. She left behind the body of her youth to impart that youth to our three kids, a sacrifice I can only observe.

She is not the same woman with whom I fell in love; she is better. She has grown. I still gaze admiringly at her lovely brown hair, and I love the bed we share. But now there is more. Her body I notice less, and her soul grows more fascinating to me. Our lives initially stood side by side, but now, like maturing dogwoods, we find that God has twisted us into one tree. How marvelous is marriage, the sacred creation of our Master.

Daily I receive the gift of looking into the blue eyes of my bride. Daily everything changes, but the beauty of her eyes remains to remind me that how I love her today will provide the answer to God's question concerning the future.

How will I love her then? May God enable me to love her yesterday, today, and tomorrow with the only love worthy of her affection. As Christ loves His church, so let me love my bride.

CHAPTER THREE

THE GOOD, THE BAD, & THE MESSY

Train a child in the way he should go, and when he is old he will not turn from it (Proverbs 22:6).

Mothers Matter
by Carol L. Baldwin

I NEVER PLANNED TO BE A stay-at-home mom. In fact, I actually didn't think about being a mother until I was widowed and single at 30, and my friends were having babies and I wasn't. Suddenly, I wanted and prayed for a family.

God answered that prayer abundantly. Five years after my first husband's death from cancer, I had married a widower and had become a mother to his two young girls. Within five years we had three more girls. There was no doubt that I was a full-time mom!

It wasn't idyllic or easy, and many times I wondered about the significance of my chosen profession. No one saw all the Legos® I picked up; the lunches I packed; the clothes I washed, folded, and put away. Lots of times I asked, "Does being a mother really matter?"

Eventually, I learned some answers to this question. Maybe some of them will hit home with you.

I am a stay-at-home mom because:

• When I was overwhelmed with a kitchen floor that never stayed clean and bottoms that always needed to be wiped, a friend told me that someday one of my little ones would put her arms around my neck and say, "I love you, Mommy," and it would all be worthwhile. And she was right.

• I realized that I wanted to be the person to help mold my children's character, not another caregiver.

• My mother was there to listen to me every day after school. And 25 years later, I still remember that.

• Pushing your child on the swing at a park is part of "mother's work," as a friend taught me.

• I am an important model to my daughters of a Christian woman, wife, and mother. (That still overwhelms me.)

• Sometimes it is even fun.

• Making my child look me in the eyes when I must discipline her and then making friends with her again later is an important step in teaching her God's justice and forgiveness.

Being a good mother matters. It matters in the ironing that gets tiresome, in the constant reminders to hang up coats and put away bookbags. It matters in wiping a toddler's nose and in writing letters to a college freshman. It all matters because God says that it does.

Whatever you do, work at it with all your heart, as working for the Lord, not for men.... It is the Lord Christ you are serving (Colossians 3:23-24).

But most of all, being a mother is important because that is what God has commanded me to do (Titus 2:4-5, 1 Timothy 5:14). God's best for my children is that I am the one to work at taking care of them. That answer puts the final lid on my doubts.

A Father's Treasure
by Kevin Woody

AS I STARE AT THE ever-growing stack of bills oozing across my desk and eating into my checkbook, I wonder how I can make some more money. "Perhaps a second job," I think to myself. Then as I open the most dreaded postal parcel of all — the credit-card statement — I ask myself, "What were you thinking when you told Michelle to quit her job and stay home with the kids?" Obviously I was watching the ACC tournament when I made that decision.

Many a young father has been financially pressured or culturally manipulated into thinking that it is necessary for both parents to work. After all, without mom's check how can we provide a wonderful home, the minivan, health insurance, and the ticking time bomb of college tuition? Maybe we've asked the wrong question: It's not *how* we are going to provide, but *what* we are going to provide.

First of all, children get the most qualified and caring teacher available to them. How much would it cost you to hire a competent, loving educator to live in your home with your kids? The reality is that God can give every child that gift in the presence of his or her parents, especially in the gift of mothers. Second, because my wife serves full time at home, I know that we are making our best effort to impart God's values by word, and more importantly, by example.

Third, every day my children get the best energy, not the emotional and physical leftovers, from at least one of their parents. Fourth, the quality and harmony of our relationships deepen because of the massive amount of time that my wife spends in our home and with our kids. Quality time is important, but it can never be divorced from quantity time. Ask any kid who only sees his parents on the weekend.

As in all things for the Christian, Jesus is the example. What was so distinctive about Jesus' ministry to His twelve friends, His "spiritual children"? Certainly they learned much from His powerful teaching and amazing miracles. But what did the Sanhedrin say about Peter and John when they grilled them in the early days of the church? They saw that Peter and John were unschooled, ordinary men, and they "took note that these men had been with Jesus" (Acts 4:13). Lots of time with the Master makes a difference. Lots of time with a Christian mother can make a similar difference.

Many today say, "We just can't make it without two incomes." I think that for some that may be true, but for most the reality is that we can't maintain a certain standard of living without two incomes. Living in a larger house or apartment, driving a new car, eating out often, watching cable television — these are some of the "treasures" that may have to be laid aside for Mom to stay at home. As for my family, we've found freedom in simplicity, God's provision for the bills, and great satisfaction in the "full time" gifts my wife offers daily to our children.

❖

What Should I Do?
by Marybeth Whalen

EVERY ONCE IN A WHILE I go through a period of wondering if I should be home with my son or out in the working world earning an income and putting my college degree to use. I'm sure every stay-at-home mom goes through this at one point or another, yet it is easy to feel that I am the only person wrestling with this dilemma. Several months ago, the Lord proved to me that I am not alone...

It was a Sunday afternoon, and I was going through the classified section of the newspaper. I had seen several job possibilities and was debating about beginning a job hunt. My husband said it was my decision, and I felt confused and lost. My son had recently turned a year old. Lots of moms can't stay home for even that long, I reasoned.

Later that day I decided to clean up our bedroom to get my mind off my problems. As I sorted through some books a friend had recently returned to me, I thought about how tight our financial situation was and how nice the extra money would be. Just that afternoon my husband had informed me that we had run out of money, and he wouldn't be getting a paycheck for another week. *How will we ever buy a house?* I wondered. *How can we start saving for our son's college education when we barely have money to live?*

As I was putting the books back on the bookshelf, I happened across a book of baby names I had lent a pregnant friend. For some reason I opened the book, and there was an envelope she had slipped into the pages. Inside was a

> **When I showed my husband the check, he said, "Honey, I think God may be telling you something."**

note thanking me for giving her some baby things my son had finished using and a check for $25! Triumphantly I ran downstairs waving the check. Although it wasn't much money, it would go a long way toward buying bread, milk, and other necessities for the coming week. When I showed my husband the check, he said, "Honey, I think God may be telling you something."

The Lord was telling me something! He was reassuring me that He will always provide for us and never let us go hungry. We may not be rich — far from it — but we are rich in love and lots of family time together. Since that day, the Lord has truly blessed our family. He even made it possible for us to buy our first home. I believe that the Lord has blessed us because I am doing the best work of all... HIS!

Keep your lives free from the love of money and be content with what you have, because God has said, "Never will I leave you; never will I forsake you" (Hebrews 13:5).

Train Up a Child
by Susan Gardner

FAMILY WORSHIP IS EXTREMELY IMPORTANT, not only for the most obvious reason of glorifying God, but also because it teaches our children the importance of having Christ live in the home.

A mother should lay the groundwork in her child's infancy for a pattern that the child can carry through the rest of his or her life. If an adult's quiet time can be established, the child sees that, and it becomes a way of life. When that child goes off to college, he has 18 years under his belt of mom's helping him with his relationship with the Lord.

In the morning

When a baby is born, read Scripture to him or her in the mornings and/or at night. Give the baby a Bible to hold.

When your children are old enough to sit in a high chair, pray with them over meals. Before they can talk, you pray for them. Develop this pattern at a young age by folding their hands for them. In the mornings when they are eating, have a devotional with them. There is material available for children even at this tender age.

Many families have a morning devotional at the breakfast table. Some dads use that time to read scripture to their children. This is also a good time to have prayer requests.

Another suggestion is to have a quiet time in the morning with your children. Before they can write, have them draw a picture about God or what God has made. For example: "God made the sun. Can you draw a picture of the sun?"

Once they can read, let them begin the day by kneeling by their bed and having their own quiet time. Again, the pattern is formed early for them to pray and read a Bible book or an easy-to-read Bible. Encourage them to keep a journal. Before they can write, have them keep a picture journal. After breakfast they can share what they learned in their quiet time that morning.

Older children can share on a more in-depth level. One suggestion is to have them share three things they can apply to their life from the morning's quiet time.

In the evening

There are many different things you can do at dinner time. Of course, this depends on the spiritual atmosphere of the home.

You can get placemats that have different Bible activities on them. On a special occasion, each person can have a different activity to share around the

> *Look for mighty moments — moments throughout the day when we are aware of God working in our lives.*

table. If dad is spiritual, have him ask how the Lord has worked in everyone's life that day. Help them to see how the Lord works. Ask, "Did you witness to anyone today?" Look for mighty moments — moments throughout the day when we are aware of God working in our lives. This establishes the pattern of looking for God throughout the day.

Some fathers read character sketches. You can also use animals and nature to show God's creation. Older children can bring out godly principles (e.g., the owl can represent wisdom).

Mom can read to the children while they eat. When they are focused in on a story, eating goes much better. Biographies of great Christians are appropriate for older children, and fun little God-related stories are good for the younger ones.

Before bed

For young children, stand over the crib and read a couple of sentences from a Bible story. They may not understand, but once again you are establishing that pattern in their lives. Even a 2-year-old can sit for a couple of minutes to listen. There are many good resources available for this time.

Bedtime is also a good time to work on Scripture memory. "A Box of Precious Promises" and "Our Daily Bread" are two good resources. These are daily scriptures printed on little cards. You can put a Scripture for the week on a wipe-off board on the refrigerator and award the children a sticker or piece of candy when they can recite the verse by heart.

Sundays

Remember to keep Sundays holy. Show the children it is a special day. Our family plays Bible trivia or a simple Bible game on this day. This is a good day to share a special meal together.

Find what works for your family, and don't become overwhelmed. Know that God will lead you in what will be best for your family.

❖

Respecting the Individual
by Nancee Skipper

AS A HOMESCHOOLING MOTHER OF six, I am often asked, "How do you give your children the individual attention they need?" My husband and I sat down and discussed our philosophy, and this is what we came up with.

• **Be aware.** We feel the key is to view our children as individuals, value them as such and treat them accordingly. This, you may say, is obvious — yes, in theory, but not in practice.

Unless you have a large family, you can't imagine how many times we have heard well-meaning people say, "I don't know how you do it; but then, what's one more when you already have... " Well, I suppose that's true if you are talking about goldfish or a litter of puppies. Our awareness of the value we place on the individual *as* an individual is critical.

In a large family, children have the benefit of the constant companionship of their siblings, and for the most part they relish it. I mean, where is the hardest place to be sacrificial, kind, thoughtful, and encouraging but with your own brothers and sisters? If you can get along with them, you ought to be able to get along with the outside world. We generally put our best foot forward outside the home.

• **Be sensitive.** If you are aware of this individuality in your daily encounters with your children, you will be able to sense their times of need. If you're unsure, just ask, "How would you like to run errands and grab a bite of lunch out, just you and me?" My children seldom turn me down. When you are impressed to spend individual time with one particular child, by all means do so. Their levels of need will vary, which brings up another point:

• **Be willing.** It doesn't take a regularly scheduled outing to a fancy restaurant to satisfy a child's need for time alone with a parent. As long as you are willing to let the impromptu conversations take precedence over the shopping, your child will be content being with you, sharing your day, and their heart.

• **Be flexible.** Scheduled times of togetherness have their place, and if your family is able to pull them off, do so with gusto. But more often than not, we must seize the moment. We know that some of the most meaningful moments of caring conversation and sharing in life come unplanned... out of the blue... and probably when we're in the midst of a dozen other things. You may not accomplish all the things on your to-do list, but you have chosen what will last.

• **Be careful.** In today's "me-first" society, we must be careful that we don't encourage this sometimes-selfish "my time" attitude in our children — or allow resentment to be fostered in us because we are constantly being deprived of it.

Many moms feel it is their job to entertain their children. It's an easy trap to fall into, but what children of the '90s don't need is more scheduled events outside the home. They need routine, yes; chores, academic stimulation, "quiet times" to read and think, and lots of playing outside to develop their imaginations.

- **Be creative.** Feeding the ducks, reading a story, taking a walk, sharing a cup of tea out of your best china... these simple pleasures cost us only time and can be enjoyed without hiring a sitter or rearranging your husband's schedule.
- **Be accountable.** If you can find a true friend who will be honest with you and help you set goals for yourself in these areas we all struggle with, you will be encouraged and challenged to keep on keeping on. Most moms are not gut-level honest with a single other woman because of our pride or vulnerability, but if you've chosen wisely, she and you will have a great opportunity to support one another on this "mothering adventure."

❖

The Perfect Day
by Jeannie Marendt DeSena

BEFORE MY DAUGHTER, OLIVIA, WAS born, I knew just the sort of mom I wanted to be: creative, devout, affectionate, sunnily unflappable. My mental outline for each perfect day at home with her was as clear in my mind as a pleasant dream just upon waking — and about as tangible.

It took me seven and a half months to have my first "ideal day" — purposeful, efficient, full of smiling baby and busy wife-and-mother who adores her child, her husband, her clean kitchen floor. A day when you think to yourself, This isn't too tough! I've got a handle on things. That night I wrote in my journal, "Today was the sort of day I had envisioned every day as a mommy-at-home being."

The trouble is, these perfect days don't follow each other like one foot after the other. My second ideal day came about three months after the first. I'm waiting for another one to happen at any moment. At this pace, I'll have three ideal days in my daughter's first year. It's a good thing we mothers don't figure our success rates like batting averages.

Looking back on that day exhausts me. I played the biblical Martha, with a hint of Martha Stewart thrown in for good measure. No accomplishment seemed out of my reach. By 8:30 a.m., I had mopped the floor for my all-but-crawling daughter. I also wrote a couple of thank-you notes, visited an 84-year-old neighbor, ironed some of Olivia's outfits, and painted the cover of a cloth book I was making for her. But I wasn't tired. I felt virtuous. Serene. In command of a well-oiled household machine.

Olivia was easy to love that day. I was able to take a shower before she got up. She decided she could play on the floor at times rather than cling and be held every moment. And miracle of miracles, my little wakeful one took a nap. We listened to her music and read Bible stories. We acted silly, smiling and

> **My journal entry concluded, "This was the day I've been waiting for since I became a mother. Thank You, Lord! Thank You, thank You!"**

giggling and playing and snuggling. I felt like a really good mother, and I had fun. My journal entry concluded with this praise, "This was the day I've been waiting for since I became a mother. Thank You, Lord! Thank You, thank You, thank You!"

After a more typical day like today — when I feel a little bit guilty and a little bit frustrated and really, really happy that Olivia's bedtime has finally arrived — April 5, 1995, seems like a lifetime ago. But that ideal day was like a glimpse of Heaven on Earth. As I struggled to cook dinner tonight while Olivia cried for attention and wiped her runny nose on my legs, I couldn't have felt much farther from the ideal. But in the journey of motherhood, like the Christian one, every day we're striving.

The Supermom Syndrome
by Jennifer McHugh

SPEEDIER THAN A 2-YEAR-OLD child. More powerful than a blender. She can wash tall piles of clothes in a single load. Look up in the attic. It's a cook, it's a maid — no, it's Supermom!

Do you ever fall into the trap of being Supermom? I think I should have the perfect child, fix gourmet dinners every night, and meet my husband at the door looking like a glamorous model as Mr. Clean stands in the background with his arms folded and big smile on his face. Mrs. Cleaver wouldn't hold a candle to me!

Do you ever feel this way? I lie awake at night trying to plan how I will get all of my many tasks done as well as spend quality time with my husband and daughter. If we try to be Supermom, the kryptonite of overcommitment will kill us. We may keep up this feverish pace for a while, but eventually we are doing no task well because we are burned out.

Some Supermom symptoms are:
- Spending less quality time with God.
- Losing sight of why I stay at home.
- Putting too many things on my "To Do" list.
- Expecting my child to be Supergirl or -boy.
- Always having a spotless house.
- Being on everybody's volunteer list.
- Allowing no time for spontaneity.

What's the solution, Supermom? How can we be everything God wants us to be without getting burned out?

Each homemaker has been called to serve God in her own way. Yes, we are all homemakers, but we have different strengths. We need to go to the Lord and ask Him exactly what He wants us to be doing. When we put our Creator first and give Him our best, He will show us what we should do and where our priorities should be.

So take time with the Lord and remember why you were called to work in the home. Cut out some "To Do's"; have realistic expectations. It's okay if you haven't vacuumed today. You don't always have to look like you just stepped out of a magazine. Only one person was perfect on this earth: Jesus. Don't beat yourself up. When all is said and done, what really matters?

Ask God what He wants you to be and spend time daily talking with Him about it, and He will tell you how to be "Super" in Him.

❖

Homemaker Blues
by Janet Steddum

THIS IS A TONGUE-IN-CHEEK LOOK at an entry we'll never see in any medical text.

Etiology and Incidence

Seen in all but the rarest of women, it is the direct result of living in close captivity with one or more small children.

Symptoms and Signs

1. Central nervous system (CNS) irritability.
2. Sleep disturbances.
3. Vocal outbursts.
4. Diminished zeal to get up in the morning.

Treatment

The homemaker in this condition must have realistic job expectations (see Supermom Syndrome). There must be a concerted effort on the part of the patient to develop and maintain other aspects of her life so as not to become one-dimensional.

Possibilities include:

1. Playing musical instruments — reported to be one of the most relaxing things to do.

2. Writing — poetry, articles for *The Proverbs 31 Homemaker*, a book.

3. Performing community service — adult literacy centers, crisis pregnancy centers, the local church, urban ministries, public schools.

4. Continuing education — local universities, community colleges, parks and recreation art/dance classes.

5. Reading — quality fiction (with restrictions on paperback pulp) and non-fiction. The local library is an excellent place to take a mommy break.

6. Exercising — a direct correlation exists between the physical and emotional states. Can be as non-complicated as strolling children at a fast pace.

7. Doing hands-on projects — anything involved in creating: coloring, painting, crafts.

8. (Not optional) Having a vibrant, daily relationship with God.

9. Enjoying fellowship — with women in similar condition as well as those who have gained the victory.

Prognosis

Excellent as long as patient is in compliance with treatment.

❖

The Overscheduled Family
by Meg Avey

*I*S YOUR CALENDAR BIGGER THAN your refrigerator? Do you pass yourself on the road? Do your children eat more meals in the car than at the table? If you answered yes to any of these questions, you may have an overscheduled family.

When you feel you must put your family in as many, if not more, activities as your neighbors or friends, you are the victim of parental peer pressure.

It may be time to do a family check on all those extra activities. Here are a few pointers.

- Pray for discernment and guidance for each child. Ask yourself: Is this an activity the child wants or something you always wanted?
- Limit each child to a maximum of two activities at a time. This helps the child to make decisions and keeps you from needing a social director.
- Check your children's physical, emotional, and spiritual well-being. Are they overtired, cranky, or overwhelmed?
- Postpone some events. "Maybe next year we can add ballet, but for now we will do soccer and art classes."

Not every activity needs to be outside the home. Consider scheduling time for family fun that requires no uniform, no carpooling, and no extra cash outlay. Relax and let kids be kids. You're the parent; you set the pace.

❖

Punishment or Discipline?
by Michelle Woody

WHEN I IMAGINED HOW EXCITING it was going to be to have children, I thought of holding, hugging, laughing, having fun, and teaching them about Jesus. After our daughter, Salem, was born, all we could think about was taking care of that precious life.

Three months later, when the doctor told me about the *new* life inside of me, I began to panic. My husband and I had wanted children close together, but a year apart? Surprise doesn't begin to cover how I felt when I heard two heartbeats!

At six months I delivered two boys, Caleb and Grant. I existed for several months knowing I was home alone — no job, no friends, no help, and no hope.

I kept telling myself things would get better. I felt resentful, exhausted, and angry.

What happened to my fun and laughter? This frustration showed itself in bursts of yelling, popping hands, and giving time-outs. I was not prepared for the anger I felt toward my children. I lost control over silly things. As one woman stated, I was in the R & R mode: ranting and raving. So I did what

> *I was not prepared for the anger I felt toward my children. I lost control over silly things. As one woman stated, I was in the R & R mode: ranting and raving.*

every Christian mom would do: pray, read James Dobson books, pray some more, ask other moms if they experienced these feelings, etc.

These measures would pacify me for a while, but I found myself still having the problem. I began to ask myself the question, "Where is all this coming from?" I grew up in an abusive home but felt that God had healed that area of my life — so why so much anger? I learned that when I became a Christian, I was "a new creation; the old has gone, the new has come" (2 Corinthians 5:17). My old self was hanging from the fender of the car, and I could hear the thumping but never got out to find out what it was.

God showed me I was wrong in my thinking concerning discipline. Here's what I learned: God's chastisement is never punitive, it is always corrective — yet mine was punishment. Consider the difference.

- Punishment is reactionary; correction is creative and controlled.
- Punishment is done with my frustrations in mind; correction is done with the children in mind.
- When you punish, you represent yourself; when you correct, you represent the Lord.

• When you punish, you confuse discipline; when you correct, you sharpen discipline.

• My discipline is to be motivated by an effort to help my children do right rather than to punish them for doing wrong. That effort will result in children who are able to discipline themselves.

After confessing my sin and tackling my problem, I began to see progress in my attitude and my kids' obedience. I saw that my expectations of my children were too high. Much of my anger occurred when I was in a hurry. God's way of dealing with this mess is with a gentle, kind, and loving word. God had to heal me inwardly. He is faithful in transforming anger to His peace.

Am I living on the edge? You bet! I am constantly moving, constantly praying, constantly changing (diapers, of course). And you know what? It is rewarding and satisfying.

❖

Accidents Happen
by Meg Avey

IT WAS A SUNNY, ALMOST-SPRING Saturday, and we decided to check out the little town just north of our house. Known for antiques, this quaint area would be a fun place to stroll around and spend some time outside. We were new to the area and had not had the chance to explore outside our immediate neighborhood, so we were excited to see what this town had to offer. We also needed to bring some china that was broken in the move to a dealer who could fix the plates.

As we parked the car in front of the antique store, I turned to our 3-year-old and told him the rules. "No touching anything in this store, Steven. Things in here are very old and can break easily. If you disobey, you will be taken out of the store and put in time-out on the steps. Understand?" Of course he nodded yes. We entered the Victorian house-turned-antique-store and admired all of the fine china and glassware. The owners were not there to look at our damaged plates, but the salesperson assured us they could be repaired.

As we were getting ready to leave, I saw the most beautiful cut-glass bowl. It was trimmed with gold and looked as if it matched some goblets I had at home. As I turned it over to see the price, a loud crash of breaking glass filled the store. The salesperson, suspecting a car had come through the front door, ran out of the back room. My husband and son hurried over to me as I stood there, shaken and pale. Unknown to me, the bowl was two pieces. The middle part fell out but did not break. Oh, no — my luck as usual — the top of the glass display case had shattered into many pieces, falling into the antique tea cups and crystal dishes inside. But the grace of God was with me at that moment, for nothing inside the case broke, in spite of large hunks of glass falling all over the contents.

We all stood there unable to say much, just looking at the slivers of glass everywhere. Steven came to me and, putting his hand in mine, said, "Does this mean you have to go to time-out on the steps, Mom?" Noting that my knees were a little weak, I told him I was going to help clean up and then I would sit down. But since this was an accident, I did not have to go into time-out.

Later, as we discussed the incident and talked about how accidents happen, I realized that in the course of a normal day Steven is faced many times with that same feeling I had at the store. Unfortunately for him, I don't always handle these situations with the same patience and understanding I received that day. As I prayed that evening, I asked God to help me be more patient with my son. I thanked Him that nothing was broken except for the glass, and since I was paying for it, I prayed that it would not be too costly. The next day the owner called to tell me the replacement would be $39. Talk about immediate answer to prayer! I had imagined the cost to be more than $200.

Since that day, I have been more patient with Steven and allowed those daily accidents of spilled milk or dropped food to pass by without much fanfare. After all, what's a little apple juice compared to hundreds of pieces of shattered glass? In the Lord's eye there is no difference, and so it should be with me.

By wisdom a house is built, and through understanding it is established; through knowledge its rooms are filled with rare and beautiful treasures (Proverbs 24:3-4).

Building a Household
by Shirley Gray

THE BABY CRIES NON-STOP, older children are fighting, and you are almost finished preparing dinner when you realize one essential ingredient is missing. Have you had days like this? I've certainly had my share of them! No one ever said that being a full-time Mom was easy, but God does promise to see us through.

These verses from Proverbs helped me to remember that a household is *built* and that it takes much thought, preparation, and work. It also takes much prayer, especially on those tough days. The Lord is able to give us wisdom and understanding to be the best homemakers possible. That's just what we are... Home-*Makers!*

It is our call from God to set the tone in the home and to make it a Christ-centered one. God honors all of our efforts to build our households, even if they seem feeble to us.

The rooms of our homes are filled with precious and pleasant riches, our children. They are truly the most valuable treasures in our lives. So isn't it worth the extra special things you do to make a house a home?

❖

DEAR LORD, HELP ME TO get through those tough days that sometimes seem endless. Give me wisdom and understanding to be the best Home-Maker I can be. Help me to make my house a Christ-centered home for my husband and my children. Show me that being a homemaker is a great privilege and honor. **Amen.**

SpaghettiO® Stains
by Kevin Woody

AS I SAT DOWN TO rest the other night, my pants reminded me of an important lesson. Gazing across the legs of my newly ironed, soft blue chinos, I discovered small orange splatters of SpaghettiOs®. I had hoped to wear these pants to work a few more times before the next cleaning. During dinner, however, one of my compassionate children had taken the time to hug me around the legs, leaving behind the evidence of his affection.

The lesson? Love requires that we get messy. Like SpaghettiOs, love leaves all kinds of marks on us. Involving ourselves in the lives of others requires that we get messy from time to time. Listening to a long-winded story that's totally irrelevant may be one of the ways that you get messy. Responding to a call for help just as you prepare to relax, or driving your neighbor to the repair shop that's not on your way — whatever the case, love requires that we get involved in the difficulties, routines, and problems of others.

We do want to love people, even people who are hard to love. But are we willing to care with actions that don't meet our agenda? We're eager to invite someone to a Bible study or discuss spiritual issues at lunch, but how do we feel about listening to their concerns, helping them with problems that don't lead to church meetings, or spending time in places that are different from what we expect?

Jesus is a messy God; He's always hugging His dirty kids. He slept in a smelly boat, touched the rotting skin of the leper, and wore the tears of a prostitute. Today, He is just as willing to get messy in the problems of divorce, the squabbles of the office, and the tears of the broken-hearted.

Loving others means getting messy. Enjoy your SpaghettiOs.

Makin' Memories
by Nancee Skipper

Four impish boys and
one pixie girl,
These are the wee ones
who make up my world.

Full of surprises,
questions, and dreams,
Limitless energy
to pursue endless schemes.

Giggling, teasing,
fussing, and noise,
Chattering continually
from my girl and my boys.

Seldom, if ever,
does silence reign here,
But neither will loneliness
be something to fear.

I know I will miss them,
for time hurries on.
My girl will be grown,
my boys will be gone.

And then my old house
will be neat as a pin.
Except for the memories
all cluttered within.

For time will not rob me
of one precious day,
Since deep in my heart
I have tucked them away.

And then when it's quiet
I'll relive our joys,
Those years I spent raising
my girl and my boys.

CHAPTER FOUR

WORDS FROM THE WISE

Likewise, teach the older women to be reverent in the way they live, not to be slanderers or addicted to much wine, but to teach what is good. Then they can train the younger women to love their husbands and children, to be self-controlled and pure, to be busy at home, to be kind, and to be subject to their husbands, so that no one will malign the word of God (Titus 2:3-5).

We Need Naomis!
by Jennifer McHugh

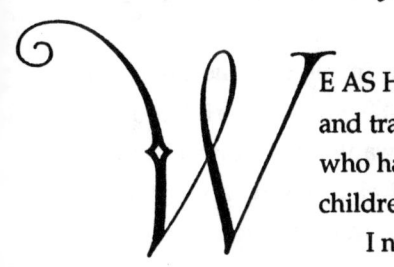

WE AS HOMEMAKERS NEED ALL the encouragement and training we can get! We need to learn from women who have experienced the challenges of raising children and going through the struggles of marriage. I need training on all of the above issues, from loving my family to being self-controlled and especially being subject to my husband. Older women can really counsel us in these areas, and most importantly, this instruction comes from God's word.

I know that somewhere there are older, godly women who are willing to encourage us. Our society moves around so much that we don't always have mothers and grandmothers nearby to encourage us the way our grandmothers did.

If you don't have a Naomi in your life, pray that the Lord will provide someone to encourage you. Look in your church or local Bible study to find someone to fill those shoes!

❖

From the 'Mentee'
by Jennifer McHugh

A HANDFUL OF OLDER WOMEN HAVE influenced my life through the years. Obviously, the most important is my own mother. Recently, I also asked the Lord to bring forward another woman with the characteristics in Proverbs 31 from whom I could learn. He answered my prayers a couple of months ago.

Right after Thanksgiving when my younger daughter, Mary Madison, was released from the hospital after recovering from a kidney infection, I came home exhausted to a place that looked like it had seen a worse week than I had. My baby was still very ill and needed quite a bit of attention. I was unable to get caught up on anything.

A friend suggested I ask a young girl to come in and give me a hand in setting the house right side up. I met Reba, and she was wonderful! Reba told me how she admired homemakers and that she wanted to be one. Her mother had raised (and still is raising) six children, and Reba couldn't speak highly enough of her. What touched me were the values, morals, and love for Christ this girl possesses. I asked to meet her mother.

I quickly learned why Reba is so special. Her mother might as well have Proverbs 31 printed across her chest. Mrs. Wilson committed to come to my home every week and help me in any way she could. She is teaching me to sew, how to organize my days, and many other practical homemaking ways, but more important, she is teaching me to become a godly parent by depending on Christ. She can relate to my mishaps and laughingly shares some of her own. Burned dinners, embarrassing moments with children, and mistakes along the way are as much a part of her life as they are a part of mine. She is someone with whom I can really share my heart.

How did she get so smart? She learned from her mother. Her mother taught her to pray, trusting the Lord for all her needs — whether it was for a parking space, food for the family, money for a hospital bill, or wisdom in raising the children.

When Mrs. Wilson tries to thank her mother, she just smiles and says, "If I did anything right in raising you, God did it in spite of me." It certainly is God who works any righteousness in us.

I will often ask Mrs. Wilson, "How can I help my daughter get through this?" or "Why am I not a better, more patient mother?" Her reply is a living

> *She is teaching me how to sew, to organize my days, and, most of all, to be a godly parent.*

example of giving every little detail to her Lord, Jesus Christ. I have learned a lot about becoming a better homemaker over the past couple of months, but I am beginning to really understand that my relationship with Christ is more than a morning quiet time: It is a minute-by-minute walk with Him throughout every day.

God puts wonderful women into our lives when we ask Him to. Thank you, Mrs. Wilson, for teaching me to be a godly wife and mother. Thank you, Sue Rudolph, my mother, for being the kindest, most wonderful mother anyone could ever ask for. I love you both!

From the Mentor
by Ruth Ann Wilson

WANTED: OLDER WOMEN TO MENTOR YOUNGER WOMEN. Do you qualify?

If you saw a new mother struggling to change a diaper and you had successfully changed thousands (or so it seemed), could you give an encouraging and helpful hint or two? If you heard a new bride lamenting the task of trying to get dinner on the table every night (with all the food cooked and served warm), could you give a few "Old Faithful,"quick and easy recipes?

I don't want to turn anyone off before you have a chance to read beyond "mentor." What an intimidating word! I wonder if that is why so many older women don't want to mentor younger women. Or could it be the word "older" that makes them decline? I don't think of myself as a mentor, just a friend. I certainly did not (and still don't) have all the answers; however, I do know the One who does. I am willing to share what has and has not worked for me.

On some occasions in the past, mothers have called me or asked to meet with me. Sometimes these initial contacts developed into weekly visits. I began to see a need for just plain-old time together — friendship. Years ago, extended families lived closer together and visited more often. Questions that arose about housekeeping, children, and motherhood would be answered quickly over a cup of coffee or during many other family gatherings.

Have you ever had a day when everything goes wrong, you wake up late, the car won't start, the roast is raw, and you have company coming? Have you ever felt like the title of Barbara Johnson's book, *Where Does a Mother Go to Resign?* Well, I have. In fact, just yesterday was one of those days. Even though my children are older, it is not any different for me. As a mentor, I share various incidents — the good, the bad, the ugly — and I am reminded myself of God's faithfulness to bring us through these times (Ecclesiastes 4:9-10).

If we saw someone stumbling, we wouldn't hesitate to reach out and keep her from injury. Mentoring is the same thing, so why do we stay silent and stand back when we know how to help another woman? We so easily get caught up in how we feel about ourselves. If you dare to reach out in this area, you may discover the satisfaction and fulfillment you were lacking and looking for elsewhere. Some of God's most precious blessings are realized when we trust and obey.

WANTED: EXPERIENCED WOMEN TO MENTOR INEXPERIENCED WOMEN. Do you qualify?

❖

That First Grandchild
by Sue Rudolph

THE SUN WAS SETTING, AND I remember thinking that the colors were especially radiant. I was driving the 150 miles to help my daughter and son-in-law for a few days with their brand new baby daughter. My first grandchild! As I admired the sunset, I thanked God for giving me this special blessing.

I must admit I was apprehensive when I first heard of the pregnancy. Could this young couple afford the cost of raising a child? Would the baby be healthy? On the other hand, I was excited to welcome this new little person into the family. What would he or she be like?

When I arrived at their house, Mother and Father were on the bed watching the baby. They were not sure what to do with her, so they just lay there and waited. They were waiting for Grandmother to come and take care of everything.

I remember bringing my first child home from the hospital and being overwhelmed at the responsibility of caring for that helpless little creature. I could understand their feelings and the look of relief on their faces when I walked into the bedroom. It was great to be needed.

The next few days and nights were busy. There were clothes to wash, food to prepare, and visitors to welcome. Most of all, there was a beautiful little girl to hold and love.

This memorable event happened more than three years ago, but thinking of that time always brings feelings of happiness and pride. Number-two grandchild is due in three months. No doubt I will have many of these same emotions, but it's hard to imagine anything more precious than that first grandchild.

❖

I Saw You Today
Anonymous

I SAW YOU AT THE GROCERY store today. Oh, you didn't see me... You wouldn't have known me anyway — for I am a stranger to you. But there you were in your slacks and T-shirt, pushing your little girl in the cart, groceries piled around her. You went down the aisle choosing the items on your carefully planned list (I bet you're having to watch your budget!). I stopped myself at the other end of the aisle and, without your awareness, I watched you.

You chatted back and forth with your little one and then impetuously reached over and placed a light kiss of affection upon her little precious cheek.

Quietly I lifted my heart to the Lord and thanked Him for you and asked Him to bless you.

I left you then and continued my own shopping only to see you again down the next aisle. This time your long, lovely hair was tied in a ponytail and you wore neat shorts and sandals. Your little boy sat in the top of the cart with his older brother holding down the bottom rack. As you rushed down the aisle, I heard you tell them they could set up the swimming pool on the deck when you got home if they promised to be good.

Again you were unaware you were being watched... but I quietly observed and again lifted you and your family to the Lord.

No, you don't know me — neither do I know you, but I love you and I admire and respect what you are doing.

For you see, I am an older woman. My years of living your lifestyle have long since passed. In fact, I have grandchildren the ages of your children. I do remember those years of never-ending demands — children, husband, housework, all the things that now consume your every waking moment. I also remember struggling with the feelings of uselessness, the moments of wondering if anyone ever appreciated my many sacrifices, or even noticed. I remember that there would be days, and sometimes weeks and months, when I would completely forget my purpose of staying at home with my children.

I suppose your "stand" to be a stay-at-home mom must meet with a greater lack of understanding today than mine did many years ago... because today you are in the minority. Society tells you it is important for you to be in a career that is self-fulfilling. It tells you to keep up with the Joneses, that every home needs two incomes to survive.

Yes, society is against you... but the good news is, God is for you!

I watched you today and you did not know... but guess who else is watching. If watching you gave *me* warm fuzzies, just imagine how the Lord must feel! Oh, my dear lady, God loves you so much! How you warm His heart. Your decision is exactly His plan.

I think He would say to you, "My child, my beloved daughter, you are so precious to me. I love you so deeply that I have entrusted to you my very greatest responsibility and honor of discipleship: that of being a mother. You are the pastor of a "great," even if small, congregation. I have placed my dearest possessions into your hands, my little babes. Care not if those around you understand or appreciate... only look up to Me. I am always and forever watching over you, as you tenderly and lovingly watch over them.

"Be not discouraged, for I am with you."

And from me to you — thank you. You are paving the way, by your example, for a new generation with morals and values that have long been displaced and forgotten. You are our hope for tomorrow... our shining star on the horizon.

You may see your task as mundane drudgery at times, but I see you as the warriors on the battlefront — as Sarah, Hannah, Esther, Mary, Martha — God's chosen handmaidens. I see you as saints!

❖

Helping Each Other
by Cheryl Bessett

HOW MANY TIMES HAVE WE sat back and watched a young mother with her child and thought, "She looks like she could use some help," without getting up to offer? There are so many strange people out there from whom we feel we must protect our little ones, that we forget our sisters in Christ are there to help — or may need help themselves.

I was sitting on my couch reading a letter from a college friend of mine, and my heart broke when she said that no one in her church has ever offered to hold her baby while she attends a quick ten minutes of prayer on Sunday mornings. I, too, have a young baby, and I have encountered the same thing. More startling is the fact that the little old ladies at the grocery store have, in fact, offered more "help" than the people in my church! This could be passed off as a "denominational thing" or a "demographic thing," except I hear this all the time.

As mighty women of God, we should be helping one another — especially we stay-at-home moms, who aren't given the opportunity for adult conversation on a regular basis or are too busy trying to figure out where we are before we can even start talking about anything other than the kids!

I felt so much for my friend; I know that just this past Sunday, I watched a new mother pack up her things and leave her pew needing the quiet ministry of God's worship much more than even I thought I needed it. I (reluctantly) asked her after the service if I could hold her little one for a few minutes while she drank some hot tea and ate a doughnut with her husband and some friends. I thought she would look at me like I fell out of a tree, as I was remembering my reaction to a woman at the grocery store just a few days before. To my *joyful* surprise, she accepted my offer, and I had the opportunity to hold her little 3-month-old.

Immediately the feeling came flooding back to me of when my own rambunctious 2-year-old was so tiny and gurgling. I also remembered how it felt to have her cry during conversations just as we had finished the baby questions and were on to real adult conversation. I smiled at the baby's mother,

> ***After the service, I asked a new mother if I could hold her little one while she drank some hot tea. The look of relief on her face after only a ten-minute break from her baby made me realize how much I had forgotten.***

who was standing just close enough to be seen but not close enough to be heard. The look of relief on her face after only a ten-minute break made me realize how much I had forgotten already!

It is different at church than at the grocery store, as it should be. Maybe the next time you feel hesitant to offer your help, offering is exactly what you should be doing! This simple and free way to help another mother can make a big difference.

The Value of Friendship
by Marybeth Whalen

WHEN I HAD MY FIRST child two-and-a-half years ago, I was filled with many emotions: fear, joy, anticipation, elation — and loneliness. After my husband returned to work and the relatives all went home, I settled into life with my baby and realized I was lonely. Being with my son was fulfilling and I loved having him, but he slept a lot, and when he was awake he wasn't much of a conversationalist. I had no friends with children since all my peers were still out in the working world pursuing careers. They all tried to be interested in my new life as a mother, but sleeping schedules and breast-feeding problems were not subjects that held their attention for longer than a few minutes' phone conversation.

Knowing it wasn't my friends' fault that we didn't have anything in common didn't help me feel any better. I began to think that maybe I would be better off at work. Then I would remember my resolution as a young girl to be a homemaker and care for my family. That resolution, and my husband's steadfast support, kept me home during those quaky first months as a stay-at-home mom. However, my loneliness still did not go away.

Lord, I began praying, please send me a friend to help me get through these lonely days. A friend who is a mother, who shares my interests, who has a husband like mine, who wants to be home with her children, and who is a Christian. Tall order? I knew it wasn't for the Lord! I began going out more as my son got a little older, and I trusted that the Lord would send that person my way.

Although it didn't happen right away, slowly I began meeting other mothers. I got involved in a secular mothers' group and met moms through play groups and meetings. A friend introduced me to *The Proverbs 31 Homemaker,* and I grew more confident about my roles as a homemaker and mother with each issue I received. I found a Christian mothers' group and was able to attend an evening Bible study, monthly meetings, and fun outings with other moms and kids. My husband and I bought our first house, and suddenly I had neighbors who stayed home like I did. The Lord had answered my prayers in abundance!

Of all the mothers I have met since those early days of my personal journey as a mother, several friends stand out in my mind as being the answer to those desperate prayers. In different ways, they have taught me about being a good mother, a good homemaker, and a dear friend. It is funny the ways the Lord sends people into your life. The things that seem to "just happen" end up being part of His divine plan.

Every minute I spend with these women and the more I learn about them, the more I realize that He meant for us to find each other and to become friends. In our own ways, our friendship has allowed us to grow into the kind of mothers the Lord wants us to be. And so, to these special women, thank you for marathon phone conversations, for brainstorming sessions, for long visits over hot cocoa, for listening to the bad days, and for cheering on the good days... thank you for your friendship. And to our blessed Lord, thank you for teaching me the value of friendship.

❖

Donna Otto: Mentors for Moms
by Marybeth Whalen

*I*T IS WITH MUCH PRIDE and excitement that Donna Otto speaks about her "Mentors for Mothers" program. The author of *The Stay-at-Home Mom, Get More Done in Less Time,* and *Between Women of God: The Gentle Art of Mentoring,* Otto began "Mentors for Mothers" to answer the need of younger mothers to be ministered to by older women who have raised families and have valuable experience to share. Otto wants to encourage more women to enjoy this benefit of aging. Too many older women, she said, are too busy denying their age by doing aerobics and going back to work or school to take time to share with younger women who need their insight.

Otto's "Mentors for Mothers" program brings these experienced and less experienced women together. This program meets through a host church for 24 weeks and follows a program based on Titus 2:3-5. It covers four six-week sessions titled "My Self," "My Mate," "My Children" and "My Mansion," with the pivotal lesson being the ministry of motherhood. Participants are taught by a leader and then break off into mentor/mom pairings for discussion. They are matched at random, but Otto said the Lord really honors the needs within each pairing. The only requirements are that participants attend each session and that the mentor love Christ, since some of the moms don't have a relationship with God when they begin the program.

Otto feels that a mentor's commitment to Christ is the biggest qualification for the program. "If a mentor has chosen Christ as her first step," she said, "then all the other steps in her life will be ordered by Him."

The mentor must also be available and committed to sharing her life with another woman. This sharing between women is the core of the program. As would be expected, many of the mentors and moms grow very close, continuing their relationship even after the program ends. More than one mom's children call the mentor Grandma, an answer to prayer for many women who live far from family.

In many situations, both mentor and mom are blessed by this program. Otto tells of Grandma Sybil, a beautiful singer who still gets calls at night from her mom's children with requests to sing them to sleep. Another mom began the program with her life in shambles and her physical appearance reflecting it. At the banquet on the last day, she showed up bright and clean, wearing a floral print dress; she stood and said of her mentor, "I don't use the word 'friend' very often, but ____ is my friend." Otto also tells of a mentor, Mabel, who lost her spouse during the program and found that the closeness she shared with her mom was instrumental in her grieving process. Those two women are still close three years later.

"Women talk in a different language; they communicate from the heart," Otto said. "They have common needs and struggle with common problems. Each woman has what the other one needs. For the older woman, she finds hope in the next generation. For the younger woman, she just loves that the older woman survived; that her child loves the Lord and her and that her marriage survived."

❖

Wild, Wonderful Becky Tirabassi
by Jennifer McHugh

BECKY TIRABASSI HAS WRITTEN A prayer journal and more than a half-dozen books, speaks across the nation on the importance of prayer, and has several Christian exercise videos on the market. But of all her accomplishments, her commitment to the Lord and dedication to spending time with Him every day are what I find most admirable.

She told me that if I spend one hour a day with the King, my life will be changed forever. I asked her how she dealt with those dry, desert times in her

Role models for today

Becky Tirabassi's newest book is *Being a Wild, Wonderful Woman for God* (Zondervan Publishing House). She said the book grew out of the frustration she felt when she realized that the role models for today's Christian women are from a very different generation and experienced different lifestyle choices. "We aren't the 1950s women," she said. "We are married and are moms and evangelists." She says the '90s Christian woman is powerful, strong, loving, and giving. She makes choices and considers how they will affect other people, not only herself.

walk with God. She said, "Jennifer, I'll be honest with you. I haven't had a dry time since I have been able to write and journal my prayers. I can assess this on a daily basis. The devil doesn't get an opportunity to steal away that time." Whew! What a statement for the Lord! She shared that she has consistently spent this time with God for more than 10 years.

You know my next question: "Yeah, but how do you have that with small children?" She told me about a friend who had her quiet time during her baby's nap. Nothing interrupted that hour — not the phone, not the laundry. Nothing. When baby number two came along, she stuck with it. Her friend now has children ranging in age from 1 to 6, and she continues her daily time with God. She has her priorities straight. Tirabassi makes a daily appointment with God in her appointment book. She also has an optional plan in case her original one gets messed up.

Talking with Becky Tirabassi was like talking to a good friend, she was so real and down-to-earth. I could tell just by the way she talked about "the King," how in love she is with our Lord. I call Becky a '90s Proverbs 31 Woman.

❖

A Conversation with Marilyn Quayle
by Lysa TerKeurst

MARILYN QUAYLE PUT HER LAW career on hold during her husband's tenure as Vice President of the United States. Although she was criticized for making her profession take a back seat to her family, she felt it was important to support her husband and to make her children a priority.

I had a chance to interview Marilyn Quayle recently at a seminar in West Virginia. She was polished yet personable, very attractive yet not flashy, and she treated our interview as if I were Barbara Walters preparing for a national television special. What a moment in time, to be carrying on a conversation with a woman not only known worldwide today but who will be in my children's history books. Yet with all of her credentials and her high profile, she is a real person, just like you and me, complete with hurts, heartaches, and daily struggles. She loves and prays to the same God we do, and leans on Him for strength and guidance.

Here is an excerpt from our conversation.

Q. How can homemakers across America make a difference?

A. There are certain rights people have, but with rights come responsibilities. We seem to understand the rights part, but the responsibility part is fading away because so many young children are being literally raised during their formative years in a day-care situation. They may be tended to there, but their soul is not being ministered to. That's totally different. That's where homemakers make a difference.

Children learn by example and the time spent with the parent — not just sitting down and reading to them and those kinds of things, but following mom around and see how she approaches every situation. They see what rules she lives by; these are really the lessons they are going to carry into their adult lives. So really the role that a homemaker has in rearing her children is more important than anything.

Q. What are your views on being a homemaker?

A. Through the 16 years that Dan and I were in public service, I learned that it's not just important for an individual to strive to be the best; being the best is a commitment to achieving the highest potential in each human being. The person who becomes the best is also the person who wants his own family, community, and country to be the best and is willing to sacrifice to make that happen.

Over the years I've been criticized, to say the least, by certain members of the feminist community for giving up my law practice when it was finally making money to help my husband and my children. Though I knew I was very blessed to have a choice, I never apologized for doing either. One thing I found, even though I was a "wife of" — I was respected on Capitol Hill because I was well prepared and did my job. The lack of a paycheck didn't matter. I learned that if you get the job done, you will be respected no matter what your title.

As a mother, I did my share of room mothering like many of you, and I did a lot of play directing throughout my children's elementary school years — all with the same philosophy: If it's worth doing, you do your best. The payoff came to me in little ways: with hugs after sixth-graders performed Shakespeare plays and a young boy coming up to me and saying, "Mrs. Quayle, thanks for making us work so hard. This is the best thing I've ever done." That child will go though life knowing that the best is only accomplished through hard work.

You never know with the little things you do, what kind of impact that have. Just being a true and loving American trying to make a difference made a bigger difference than I could have ever dreamed. So, when you're thinking you may be "just a housewife" or "just a volunteer," every little thing you do does make major consequences. You may never know, but the impact will be just the same. There are limits to what government alone can contribute to our

---

"I learned that if you get the job done, you will be respected no matter what your title."

MARILYN QUAYLE

---

prosperity, but there is no limit to the accomplishments of an individual fired with enthusiasm and committed to an idea.

Q. How can homemakers make a difference in politics?

A. Don't ever say, "I can't change anything; it's beyond me." You have to be willing to give of yourself in order to get the kind of government you want, with the ideas and values you believe in. It's time we all fought back and said, "Yes, I will volunteer. I want the person in office who mirrors my beliefs and will put this country back on the right track." Only 27 percent of the voting population is voting. A lot of changes could be made if we could get more people involved in the electoral process.

Making Time for Yourself
by Nancee Skipper

DO I EVER GET ANY time to myself? The answer is yes — maybe not as much as I want, but as much as I need (more about that later). If you mean regularly scheduled blocks of time, that depends...

Different phases of life lend themselves to different "free times" for me. Most days, I require all of my six children to have a quiet hour or nap time, depending on age. This is also *my* quiet hour or nap time, depending on my energy level.

Also, I have been blessed with a supportive husband who is willing to let me get away whenever the pressures mount. Once or twice a month, I meet with two other moms for unburdening, accountability, and prayer. I'm usually not home until after midnight, but my husband has never complained. Really!

He is also the one who strongly encourages me to write or speak to different groups when I get the opportunity; and though it sometimes takes more time to prepare for these events, it is extremely enriching to me. It's my outlet. Writing and speaking about mothering or homeschooling force me to focus on *why* I'm doing this. It validates my choices, and that's a real shot in the arm. So find your creative outlet, whether it be crocheting, cross-stitching, making wreaths, decorating your home, journaling, painting, or whatever. Of course you won't be able to do this every day, or every week, or even every month, but it's something that's yours when those brief spots of time are available, and someday you will be able to devote more time to it. Creative expression has recuperative powers.

I also believe in "mini vacations"... like a walk alone, a romantic old video, a good book at the end of the day. Rewarding myself in little ways always helps, as long as it's not fattening. Sitting quietly with a cup of coffee for a few minutes and taking a look at an old photo album show me how quickly time is passing and how soon (yes, soon) I will have worked myself out of a job.

There have been times when I had a regularly scheduled aerobics class and it was great, but that's not an option now. A brisk walk outdoors is sufficient.

Every three or four months, my ever-sensitive mother singlehandedly and of her own free will volunteers to keep our crew for a couple of nights so my husband and I can get away. She lives two hours away in the lovely mountains of North Carolina, so we trade houses. Inexpensive and refreshing.

Caution! When you do have choice moments of time, use them wisely. I've made the mistake of picking up the house, balancing the checkbook, folding laundry, and running a quick errand all in one rare "free" afternoon. I end up more exhausted than when I started. Sometimes this can't be helped because things are too messy for me to relax, but choose what will refresh your spirit.

More important than any of the above is my need for a daily, early morning "quiet time." Even my feeble, distracted, half-hearted attempts can recharge my batteries and give me a gentler spirit. Elisabeth Elliot's ministry through books and radio (though I seldom hear it) has convicted me and encouraged me in the area of dying to self. (Not the kind of thing a '90s woman wants to hear, but oh, how we need it.)

You see, even after six children, I am still a very selfish character, but I am even more certain of God's sovereignty in my daily life. Because I believe my time is in His hands, I'm learning that I must daily die to my demands for:
- my time,
- my plans,
- my desires.

Mothering involves daily sacrifices of:
- our bodies,
- our energies,
- our talents.

But if we can make this a "glad surrender" of self-abandonment, self-donation; if we can willingly see that we are to do this unto the least of these as unto Him; if we can see these mundane chores as spiritual acts of worship to our Lord... my, how that elevates the tedium of life.

CHAPTER FIVE

OF PURSE STRINGS & APRON STRINGS

"Provide purses for yourselves that will not wear out, a treasure in heaven that will not be exhausted" (Luke 12:33).

My Hunk of Burning Love
by Lysa TerKeurst

A COUPLE OF WEEKS AGO, MY husband and I had some friends over for a cookout and Bible study. While I was inside frantically trying to prepare the food, tidy up the house, put my child to bed, and greet my guests with a smile, my husband was outside firing up the grill. We were running a little tight on time, so my husband decided to quicken the process. He went to the garage in search of something to help speed up the fire. He found... gasoline.

Things definitely sped up, so much so that our garage door wound up on fire. Luckily the dog's water dish was handy to remedy the situation.

Looking back on that day makes me chuckle but also reminds me of an important lesson learned. How many times do we hurry through things because of lack of proper planning, causing a crisis? Some days I seem to do all right, but more times than not I'm running late, rushing through activities, and dropping at the end of a day spent catching up. There has to be a better way!

Where do we end this cycle? The Bible offers many good suggestions.

In Genesis 41:28-36, Joseph interprets Pharaoh's dream to be a survival plan for the next 14 years. They had to plan and properly manage in order to save their nation from famine. Granted, we aren't in danger of a famine, but when we properly plan ahead, it can help alleviate worry. Matthew 6:34 says, "Planning for tomorrow is time well spent; worrying about tomorrow is time

> *Don't let worries about tomorrow affect your relationship with God today. Our families need to see us as "warriors" for God, not "worriers."*

wasted" (TLB). The worrier lets his plans interfere with his relationship with God. Don't let worries about tomorrow affect your relationship with God today. Our families need to see us as "warriors" for God, not "worriers." Here are a few tips to get you started.

• **Plan your day.** Divide your activities into "must do" and "want to do" activities. Realistically assign time slots for your "must do's" and then fill in your "want to do's" accordingly. Be practical. With small children involved, the schedule has to be flexible.

• **Plan your errands.** Use a map to figure out the most efficient routes. Call ahead to make sure the store you are going to carries what you need.

• **Plan your housework.** Assign yourself certain chores for each day of the week to avoid getting overloaded.

Maybe you expert planners can give me more great tips. In the meantime, my "burning hunk of love" and I have a date to paint the garage door.

It's Not in the Budget
by Janet Steddum

*I*T HAS BEEN SAID THAT if the members of Congress want to learn how to balance the federal budget, they would do well to sit down with a homemaker who must allocate her family's limited income and ensure that all basic needs are met. Fiscal responsibility, or operating within a budget, isn't relegated exclusively to the halls of government, major corporations, or financial institutions. It begins at home with a conscientious, systematic effort to account for the spending of the family's incoming money. It culminates in a thorough understanding of the household's financial health at any given moment and allows for intelligent decision making (Proverbs 31:16,18a).

There is an abundance of instructional material on the "mechanics" of devising a budget. But really, all you have to do is take what you make and live on less. This takes discipline, determination, and a clear understanding that God's desire for us is freedom from financial bondage, not the tyranny of keeping up with the Joneses (as manifested by debt) and dealing with the accompanying anxiety.

A written budget showing where the money comes from (income) and where you want it to go (expenses) is a tool to help you establish spending priorities. When you get ready to make a purchase, you will at least know beforehand, by consulting your budget, the repercussions of that decision. (For example: If we upgrade our auto to the new and improved version, we will have to eat beanie-weenie five times a week.) Therein lies the peace.

Here are some guidelines.

1. Since it all belongs to God (Acts 17:25) and you are merely the steward or manager (Luke 12:42-48), ask Him how much of your income He wants you to use to live on and how much goes elsewhere. Elsewhere means:

• your first fruits (Proverbs 3:9) — the local church, a missionary;

• impromptu gifts for a needy family (James 2:14-17);
• savings (Proverbs 10:5, 31:21) for unexpected emergencies, such as uncovered medical expenses, a totaled car, job termination, etc.;
• a buffer to help prevent cash-flow problems.

2. Ensure that your non-discretionary expenses (i.e., housing, utilities, auto insurance, food, taxes) can be met.

3. Allocate what's left for discretionary expenses (i.e., eating out, recreation).

Note: Your expenses lie on a non-discretionary/discretionary continuum, and you must decide where they fall.

Continue to seek the Lord for direction in your finances! It isn't always easy, but there is great freedom in living within these guidelines.

❖

I Won't Make My Own Soap!
by Brent Wainscott

SHORTLY AFTER MY WIFE, BARBARA, and I were married, I examined her spending habits and realized I had a tough task ahead of me. I would have to change her preconceived ideas of what it meant to discount shop and live on a budget. Barbara informed me, in most certain terms, that she would have nothing to do with any store outside "the mall" and she was definitely not interested in making her own soap.

Do you consider budgeting or outlet shopping or even using coupons as something constricting or unpleasant? I promise you these images will pass, and you will see how much fun it can be to save money while getting a good deal. Just ask Barbara! After nearly eight years of marriage, my wife has become the queen of outlet shopping and scopes out coupons for just about everything we buy. The best part is, we still get the quality she was used to as single professional. But why pay full price when you can pay less?

Here are some of "Bargain Barbara's" money-saving, power-shopping ideas:

1. Do you take the time to mail in manufacturer's coupons, or do you think you shouldn't waste the stamp? Think again! Once you mail in a rebate coupon, you are placed on the manufacturer's mailing list for further "good deal" coupons. We get a free bag of Purina dog food about every three months because of this.

2. Don't stop using coupons just because you're on vacation.

3. The yearly Entertainment guide available at drugstores and other stores is well worth the $30 to $35. If you eat out much, you can recoup the purchase price in only two outings.

4. You have to comparison-shop before hitting the clothing outlets (some prices aren't so great, but an Izod men's shirt costing $40 at a department store typically will be $14 at the outlets). Barb's favorite outlets are in Pennsylvania (no sales tax), and the most expensive are in Texas and Tennessee, with 8 to 8.5 percent sales tax.

5. Check the Wednesday and Thursday newspaper supplements for grocery coupons, and shop on Friday for free tastings and manufacturer's coupons.

6. For groceries and other goods, shop three different stores to compare prices, and get different specials from each store.

If you have a freezer and can buy in bulk, you can save when prices are low. If you want a freezer, buy one during the off-season (winter), and buy last year's model if you must have a new one.

7. Hold a garage sale and sell your older unused items. We have never made less than $80, even on a spur-of-the-moment garage sale, and have made as much as $500.

If you do crafts, try selling them at a garage sale. Who knows, you may have a part-time business! (Note: Some items might be better as a charity write-off at IRS-suggested market values.)

8. If you eat at a fast-food restaurant that has free refills, buy the smallest drink you can. I'm amazed when I see someone get a large drink (not to go, of course) and refill it, and pay 25 to 30 cents more for the same amount of drink I had. What's one more trip to the fountain? I need the exercise anyway!

9. When buying new furniture, look for sales with "one year, same as cash" payment plans, but don't overpay for the privilege. If used or slightly used/antique furniture is desired, try consignment stores; you'll be surprised at some deals if you keep you eyes open.

Try some of these suggestions and watch yourself become a savings dynamo! You, the homemaker, can greatly influence the household budget and make your priceless work at home worth even more.

Set goals as a couple, and challenge each other to save, save, save. But don't make me make my own soap or cut open the toothpaste tube for that last bit of toothpaste. It's just not going to happen.

❖

Food for Thought
by Janet Steddum

MY HUSBAND, HALF IN JEST, recommends staying home as a means of saving money. He says we get into trouble the moment we start the car. I couldn't agree more!

Here's some "food" for thought as you approach the arduous task of grocery shopping.

Goal:
To purchase the MOST NUTRITIOUS FOOD

at the LEAST COST

in the LEAST AMOUNT OF TIME.

Strategy:

1. Plan meals a month at a time (yes, you can). Benefits include: less stress from last-minute "scrambling" for a meal; better balance and variety; and less cost and waste.

2. Create a shopping list (output of step one).

3. Shop once a month for non-perishables (two or more stores), weekly for perishables (spending less than 15 minutes in the store).

4. Create a "price book" listing the non-sale price of items you purchase

> *Create a "price book" listing the non-sale price of items you purchase regularly. This will instantly tell you which store has the best price for a given product. Using ads in conjunction with your price book, locate bargains to buy in bulk.*

regularly. This will instantly tell you which store has the best price for a given product so you can shop accordingly.

5. Use ads in conjunction with your price book to locate exceptional buys, and bulk buy these items when possible. Remember "loss leaders" (items advertised on the front and back pages of the circular, sold at a "loss," and designed to get you into the store).

6. Coupons: Easy does it! Would you purchase the product anyway? Most coupons are for "new" (read: repackaged/expensive) items.

7. Question your buying habits: "My mother always bought brand x, so I will, too." Could a generic product fit the bill? Better yet, can you do without it?

If you apply wisdom, tailoring these suggestions to meet your specific needs, you'll be pleased with the results. Go ahead and start your engines.

Winning the Grocery Game
by Janet Steddum

I AM EASILY DISTRACTED BY ATTRACTIVE or unusual displays at the grocery store. (I am not sure, but I think merchandisers want me to be so I'll part with my hard-earned cash.) So I've found that if I want to win the grocery game, I had better understand the rules! Here are a few that I have found to be cash catchers.

• **Consider store/shelf layout.** Merchandisers pay a premium to have their products prominently displayed. They know that they can increase the likelihood of having their product selected just by its position on the shelf or location in the store. Predictably, this cost will be passed on to you. Low markup items can be awkwardly placed on a bottom shelf or in an obscure corner. Competing products are not usually next to each other, so you may have to walk up and down the aisle to compare.

• **Generic vs. namebrand.** The shocking truth is that some generics are processed at the same plants as namebrands, with just a change in packaging. The real issue here, however, is not whether a generic is identical in every way to the national brand, but whether it is good enough for your family. Does the generic meet your requirements? Could you make some adjustments to your taste? To be sure, some generics are of inferior quality, but don't write one off until you're sure it won't fit the bill.

• **Avoid processed foods.** There are foods that are not in their simplest, unadulterated form. Examples include frozen foods, salad dressings, noodle/rice mixes, spaghetti sauces, and some breakfast cereals; you get the point. Processed foods are almost without exception very expensive (compared to preparing the item from its components), they contain not-so-benign additives, and they can be low in nutrition.

• **Learn to eliminate.** Just because someone hawks it, doesn't mean we need it. Manufacturers attempt to generate a demand for their products by persuading us we will somehow be better off as a result of using them. Rest assured, your kids won't think you love them less if you serve potatoes instead of stuffing.

You can already see the generation of "false demand" in the health and beauty aids industry. Now you can watch for it in the grocery store.

• **Look for unit pricing.** By reducing the price to its price per unit (ounce, pound, item, etc.), you can readily compare two packages to determine if the "economy" size really is in fact economical.

When shopping, be deliberate. Always have your list in hand and concentrate on what you're doing. This may mean going by yourself. In no time you'll be whizzing down the aisles, faster than a runaway cart, able to spot bargains from clear across the store... and saving a bundle.

❖

Eating Out for Less
by Janet Steddum

TO GET THE MOST FOR your money when you dine away from home, consider these suggestions:

1. Incorporate eating out into your meal plans. You know you probably will (unless it's not in the budget), so schedule it. This prevents you from being held hostage by restaurant row when you're tired and hungry, and the kids are screaming.

2. Survey local restaurants to determine which provide the most "performance" for the price.

Ask friends. Consider buffets where kids eat free with a paying adult, weekly "kids' night" specials, cafeterias, ma & pa restaurants, and places with few frills.

3. Get a copy of the menu beforehand (most restaurants will give them upon request) so you can analyze your choices (for nutrition, portion size, price) and have a good idea what you will order. This eliminates the pressure to order quickly — and expensively — before the waitress disappears.

4. Do lunch. Lunch menu items are almost always cheaper than the same item on the dinner menu, even for the same size portion. When the lights go down, the price goes up.

5. Drink water with your meal. Soft drinks, teas, and other beverages have the greatest markup of any menu item. Plus, you don't need the extra caffeine or sugar.

6. Challenge yourself to order less than you think you'll need. You'll be surprised how little you require to be full but not bloated. If you're not satisfied, then order again.

❖

Down-to-Earth Decorating
by Rhonda Jaynes

YOU CAN ACCESSORIZE THE ROOMS in your home without extra expense if you look at old things in a new way. Often the key to decorating on a budget is imagination. Making something out of nothing is not only economical but extremely satisfying in terms of creativity. It doesn't have to be costly to have a warm, tastefully decorated home. A little ingenuity, a few odds and ends, and a caring touch can go a long way.

Begin by searching through closets, attics, tops of cabinets, and storage areas. Your "finds" may include old books, doilies, scarves, quilts, candlesticks, or still-unused wedding gifts! You may run across objects that are potential lamps, vases, centerpieces, or artwork. The idea is to see that old or seemingly useless item as a possible "new" accessory.

Stacking old or new books on end tables among pictures, lamps, candles, or other items has become a popular decorating trend. Drape a pretty doily, scarf, or handkerchief over the edge of a table or dresser top for a special effect. A soup tureen by itself or with flowers or fruit can make a lovely centerpiece. Scraps of barn wood can make cute shelves, while old crates can serve as interesting plant stands. Your artwork can make a great conversation piece. Spray paint or faux pottery spray can turn a bottle or plastic container into a very pretty vase. Let your imagination be your guide.

Here's a case in point:

My grandmother left me some special pieces that originally came from Ireland. I didn't know what to do with them for years, but I knew I wanted to display them. Among these items were one lace curtain panel with a few holes

> *Drape a pretty doily, scarf, or handkerchief over the edge of a table or dresser top for a special effect. A soup tureen by itself or with flowers or fruit can make a lovely centerpiece.*

in it, an embroidery hoop and thimbles, three hand-woven hot pads, and an antique butter knife and spoon with pearl handles.

I chose to swag the curtain panel at my dining room window in a manner that hid the holes. I glued the hoop and thimbles to a painted burlap background and mounted them in a plain black frame. I did the same with the hot pads and silverware. These 10 x 13-inch frames hang to the left and right of this window.

I get more positive comments on these accessories than on any other in my home. The frames were from yard sales, I had the burlap on hand, and the paint was left over from the walls.

Cost-conscious decorating ideas

Here are some more ideas for free or almost-free decorating:

• To give a room a refreshing new look, try rearranging your current furniture.

• Start a file of rooms that you like. I go through old magazines and save anything that catches my eye. After doing this for a year, I learned the "style" I like the most and had a bunch of new ideas.

— Meredith Banks

• Attend home tours and open houses by local builders' associations and the Board of Realtors. Many of these homes have been professionally decorated, and they provide an endless supply of ideas that can be completed on a budget. Often, the interior designers are on hand to answer questions. While attending these home tours, I have seen people carrying cameras, notepads, and even video cameras to record ideas for later use.

• Look for classes offered at hardware stores, paint shops, wallpaper stores, and home centers. These classes are usually free and teach the latest techniques in wallpapering, sponge painting, stenciling, etc. This is a nice way to achieve a decorator look without the high price tag. Take a class with your husband and start a project together, or team up with a friend and help each other with your decorating ideas.

• Check out some books at your local library for more decorating ideas. Leslie Linsley's *Weekend Decorating*, for example, is full of quick and inexpensive ideas to update or spruce up your home.

— Marybeth Whalen

CHAPTER SIX

HOLIDAYS & EVERYDAYS

This is the day the Lord has made; let us rejoice and be glad in it (Psalm 118:24).

Every Day is Valentine's Day
by Meg Avey

WE ALL KNOW THAT VALENTINE'S Day was created by the Big Three — candy stores, florists, and card shops — but why should we limit showing our love to just one day? (Of course, after the January bills are paid, the $3.50 left over doesn't go too far.) It is possible to shower your husband and children with love by letting your creative juices flow!

Remember it is the giving, not the receiving, that counts. Don't expect anything, and you will be happy when they actually do reciprocate. And cost is not the determining factor. For instance, a small act of kindness speaks more than a 25-pound box of chocolates.

I hope these ideas spark in you the willingness to try fun and creative ways to say "I love you" to the most important people in your life.

- Get up early one morning and make personal pancakes. Make each member big pancakes decorated with hearts, funny faces, and their names. You can buy icing in small tubes or make your own.
- Cut out lots of construction-paper hearts and write on them what you love about your husband or child. Place them all over the house so when they come home they can read what is in your heart.
- Arrange a picnic lunch in winter. Spread a tablecloth on the floor and serve summer foods, right down to the frozen juice bars. Have everyone wear sunglasses and shorts.
- Mail love letters or cards to your husband's office. Spray them with perfume and sign with a lipstick kiss. Let him know what is in store for him that evening. You can bet he will not work late that night!
- Surprise your children by putting in their lunch boxes the one junk food snack they love and you hate.
- Ask for prayer requests from your family. Write them down and let them know they are being prayed for. This is a great way to share your love with them.
- Think back to L.B.K. (Life Before Kids) and re-create a great trip, holiday, or romantic interlude. Gather memorabilia from that time — souvenirs, photos, etc. Take the kids to a friend's house to spend the night (a gift for them) and revel in your love.
- Create a Fantasy Box. Have everyone write down how they would spend a day if they could do anything, and put all of the ideas in a special box. Each month or week, pull out one fantasy and try to make it come to life (within reason and budget). Use your imagination.

For example: A ski trip to Europe? Serve hot chocolate around a fireplace with everyone wearing hats and scarves. Talk about the great runs you all had, the falls you took, and the cute ski instructor.

A spaceman walking on the moon? Buy freeze-dried food from a camping store, get a book on astronomy, and learn about the universe.

Making Birthdays Special
by Jennifer McHugh

BIRTHDAYS ARE SO MUCH FUN for little ones. One of my favorite traditions in our family is the first birthday cake. The birthday child is stripped down to the diaper and placed in front of a small cake. Then he or she is free to dive in. My first daughter wouldn't touch it until we gave her a little taste of the icing. After that, look out! There was cake from head to toe! After the cake was demolished, she was scooped up inside the tablecloth and taken off to the bath. My husband's family thought the tradition a little strange, but we all enjoyed it immensely.

Here are some other birthday ideas and tips:

- Make a banner and hang it in the yard.
- Serve the birthday child a favorite meal on a special birthday plate.
- Show your child home movies of himself as a newborn, or pull out the photo album.
- Have all at the table share why they love the birthday child.
- Write your child a special letter each year on her birthday. Ask Dad to write one, too.
- Serve the birthday child breakfast in bed.
- Don't focus on the birthday party as much as celebrating the entire day with the child.

Try to have the birthday party on a weekend day before so that on the birthday itself, the focus can be on the child, not the party.

- Have a small present at the foot of the bed for the child when she wakes up.
- Most importantly, be sure to remind the child through your words and actions how important he is to the family and how glad you are that he is part of it.

Is It Just the Thought that Counts?
by Marybeth Whalen

IT IS ALMOST VALENTINE'S DAY. You are anticipating a romantic celebration with your husband, complete with dinner out for the two of you, a bouquet of flowers, and possibly a small token of his affection — a heart-shaped charm or a delicate gold chain; a special bottle of scented bubble bath and a coupon for a kid-free morning to use it; a tape of favorite songs from when you dated... the possibilities are endless in your scenario of the perfect Valentine's Day. In actuality, your husband may get the dinner and flowers part, but often the gift ends up being a letdown.

This happened to me on several occasions. I would build up the upcoming holiday in my mind, only to be disappointed when I opened my husband's trademark Ziggy card and stuffed bear! I'll never forget the Valentine's Day when we were dating and I was sure he would propose, but he didn't. Instead of an engagement ring, I received something else (I don't remember what it was), and we didn't celebrate, we ended up in an argument. He didn't even realize I was expecting an engagement ring. But the argument got us talking about the subject, and he did propose on another holiday — April Fool's Day!

The moral of this story is that I have learned the hard way not to expect a romantic gift from him unless I have hinted around at least 100 times or so. Like many husbands, mine is usually out on his lunch hour on February 13th looking for something to buy me. But he is getting better. He used to say, "We don't have the money to exchange gifts." How much money does it take to give me a Saturday to myself? To write a love letter? Many times the gifts wives treasure from their husbands don't require money, just some thought and time.

This is not to say that I am faultless in the gift-giving department. I can't tell you the number of sweaters he has received on Christmas morning. And

I'll bet he would have much preferred a morning of golf instead of those glow-in-the-dark boxers with hearts on them. It is hard to resist the commercialized, clichéd items we pass in the mall, but I am learning to.

On these special occasions, the best thing husbands and wives can do for each other is not expect anything. When selecting a gift, think of the other person's personality, likes, and dislikes. And communicate your wishes to your spouse, because no one is a mind reader!

I'm grateful for such a wonderful husband who does take my son out on Saturday mornings so I can sleep in and who takes me to a good movie every once in a while. His gift giving is improving, and so are my expectations.

Good luck this year, and tell your husband to say hello to mine on February 13th!

❖

Hatching the Easter Story
by Susan Yount and Sidney Dunlap

MOST CHRISTIANS CELEBRATE EASTER with tremendous joy, knowing that our Lord's redeeming love on the cross, His crucifixion, death, and resurrection, are our source of life now and forever. Most Christian parents desire above all else that their children know and understand the love of Christ, and accept the gift of salvation made possible through the Easter story.

Our challenge is communicating the Easter story and the awesome truths inherent in our Christian heritage in ways that our children will truly understand. Relying on the power of prayer and the Holy Spirit, we can share the Easter story using effective learning techniques.

Here is one way you can lay an Easter foundation with your children: make "Hatching the Greatest Treasure: The Easter Story in Eggs." You can use a six-egg story (which we recommend for preschoolers) or a dozen-egg story, depending on the attention level and development of your child.

To make "The Easter Story in Eggs":

1. Spray a half or whole egg carton with gold paint.
2. Glue faux jewels on the outside of the dry carton.
3. Fill the carton with plastic eggs.
4. Using a permanent marker, number the eggs 1-6 or 1-12.
5. Review the Easter story in Scripture (John 3:16, Matthew 26-28, Mark 16, John 19-20), keeping in mind ways you can illustrate the story.
6. Decide on the six or twelve points and corresponding objects from the Easter Story that will relate to each egg. (For a 12-egg story, those objects might be: a Bible opened to John 3:16; bread and a wine cup; silver coins; a soldier figurine; a crown of thorns and a square of purple cloth; a cross; a nail; a sponge; white cloth and a stone; cloves; and an angel; and emptiness.)
7. Purchase and/or make the objects.
8. Fill the eggs with the objects.
9. Write a script using the Easter story from Scripture, assigning a number to each point, corresponding object, and numbered egg.
10. Practice the story until you are comfortable... then GO TELL THE GOOD NEWS to your child or children.

Begin by saying that you are about to share the greatest treasure in all creation, the Easter story. This is a story of GRACE (God's Riches At Christ's Expense)... a story of joy. Also begin with egg No. 1 reflecting the source of this story... the Bible, God's true Word. Get excited as you share John 3:16, God's love and Jesus' desire for us to live forever with Him!

The last egg will be empty like the tomb, because Jesus lives. He rose from the dead, so we are free to love Him and other people. Be sure to wish your children a Happy Easter and give big hugs! Then invite them to tell you the story. Invite them to share the story with a neighbor, friend, or anyone else. Remember... Jesus said that a child will lead them!

Offer to share the Easter story with your child's preschool or Sunday School class, or during a children's church sermon. Educators are very receptive to the learning principles employed in Hatching the Greatest Treasure. Sharing the Easter story teaches storytelling techniques, including progression and sequencing, as well as reading cues (symbols, object association) and preparedness (sorting and classifying, if you let them explore the eggs and reassemble them). Handling the items contributes to fine muscle development. Shapes, colors, and numbers can be reinforced during egg play, and children gain verbal skills as they retell the story.

Enjoy watching your children learn the Easter story, share the Good News, and experience God's grace in many ways through this learning tool.

Caution: Young children should be supervised while handling the egg set. Small objects, sharp points, and breakable plastic present safety issues.

❖

Harried Holidays
by Jennifer McHugh

I HAVE TALKED WITH MANY HOMEMAKERS who don't exactly look forward to the holidays. Sure, they enjoy the food and (sometimes) the extra family, but the preparation often makes the holiday season a dreaded time instead of a delightful one. The added burdens of visiting relatives, cooking elaborate meals, cleaning for extra people, and coping with hyper children put stress on us.

I know that in years past, I have found myself snapping at my husband and children because things were not going my way. One Christmas Eve comes to mind. My family never went to church on this special night when I was growing up. On the other hand, my husband never spent a Christmas Eve at home; he was *always* at church. Mike loves eggnog at Christmas and had finished off our supply that afternoon. I insisted on going to church that night, and my husband reluctantly agreed.

Getting ready was crazy. I couldn't find the correct shoes to wear. We scarfed down dinner and raced out the door to get to the church on time. We arrived only to find out there was no nursery. Our daughter was 14 months old and did not sit well for an hour. We squeezed into the back of the church and attempted to listen with a squirming little one on our laps.

All of the children were called up front (ours was, of course, too little) to hear the Christmas story. The children's story was over *my* head — we couldn't see a thing sitting in the back, and Morgan was really fussy (it was past her bedtime). Mike and I ended up leaving halfway through the hour.

The only thing left on the agenda was to get eggnog so we could get on with the evening. For some reason we were driving two cars, and we followed

> *Enjoy whatever happens. If things don't go as planned, don't worry!*

each other to a half-dozen stores before going home empty-handed.

Needless to say, the evening did not go as I had planned.

It was a great learning experience. We now have our own "service" at home. We have a birthday party for Jesus and a special dinner, and we read as a family from the Bible. I still get to enjoy what I craved, giving God the glory on this special night. My husband shares in that and enjoys it at home. And we always have plenty of eggnog.

Each of us has her own traditions for November and December. During these months, please take a minute each morning (and throughout the day, if necessary) to relax. And enjoy whatever happens — if things don't go as planned, don't worry! Don't feel that you have to have everything planned and perfect for friends and family. Believe me, they will have a much better time if you are relaxed!

Also, remember your husband during the holiday season. Plan some romantic time for just the two of you. Relax in front of the fire. A happy husband makes for a happy holiday.

A New Year's Tradition
by Beth McKnight

SEVERAL YEARS AGO WE HAD a New Year's Eve party where we "prayed in" the new year. We prayed ahead of time about whom to invite. We invited a large group, many of whom did not know one another, and left it to the Lord to select the group. Just the right number of people came, and just the right blend. We gathered about 9 p.m., after church services, and had time to socialize before beginning to pray, around 10:30 or 11 p.m. We also read Scripture aloud.

After midnight, I served a light breakfast of mock cheese soufflé with fruit salad and banana nut bread. Some people left, and some stayed and talked until the wee hours.

It was a warm, positive way to begin the new year with cherished friends.

❖

A Year's Worth of Ideas
The Proverbs 31 Homemaker Activity Calendar

THE PROVERBS 31 WOMAN CONCERNED herself with building a strong relationship with her husband, nurturing her children, giving to the community in which she lived, and of course loving and serving her God. The following activity calendar offers suggestions along the same lines. It is a perpetual calendar, so projects and celebrations, while seasonally appropriate, are not tied to days of the week or to holidays that change dates, like Easter and Thanksgiving. Each month you also will find four "Sunday Specials" — ways to mark the Lord's Day as a family. Consult the calendar for inspiration when you're running dry, or to help you plan a balanced family life. It's a tool for you — enjoy it!

JANUARY

1. Start off the year by helping your child to set some goals.

2. Spend time in prayer; ask the Lord what areas in your life you should work on.

3. Make a calendar for the year with your kids. Highlight special days with stickers and markers.

4. Plan a no-cost mystery date. Mark it on the calendar; build suspense by dropping hints to your husband about the activity.

5. Make straightening the house fun. Put on some music, and try to finish a room before the song ends.

6. Family Night. Teach your little ones to play charades.

7. Make a prayer box, and encourage your kids to put requests inside. Pray daily for them.

8. Put your Christmas cards in a basket. Each night at dinner, pick one and pray for the sender as a family.

9. Bundle up and go for a brisk walk. When you get home, serve hot cocoa.

10. Find a children's story hour at a bookstore or library.

11. Draw pictures and mail them to grandma and grandpa.

12. Have a Praise Day. Teach your children a lively Christian song and make up motions to go with it.

13. Family Night. Watch a movie together. Play "movie critic" afterward, letting all tell what they liked and disliked about it.

14. Make puppets from old gloves or socks. Do a show for Daddy.

15. Make today a stay-home day — no errands, traffic, or carseats.

16. Think summer! It's beach night. Eat a picnic dinner on a blanket in sunglasses, swimsuits.

17. Take the kids to visit a retirement home.

18. Eat lunch *under* the kitchen table.

19. Family Night. Have a homemade-pizza party. Make mini pizzas with lots of toppings.

20. Write a love letter to your husband.

21. Memorize a Bible verse. Let the kids draw a picture for the verse.

22. Practice cutting on pictures from old magazines. Make collages.

23. Call a friend you haven't talked to in a while.

24. Invite the stay-at-home moms in the neighborhood to a social.

25. Celebrate Jesus' birth with a kind deed.

26. Get your husband's favorite children's book, and encourage him to read aloud at bedtime.

27. Start a journal for your child.

28. Family Night. Exercise as a family.

29. Attack a small project you've been putting off. Labeling those photos?

30. Plan your special days for February. Don't forget family nights, anniversaries, or birthdays.

31. Throw an end-of-the-month party. Bake snowman cookies.

Sunday Specials
• Plan a family worship service with favorite songs and Bible verses. Ask each person to pray aloud. • **Write a special note to thank your child's Sunday School teacher for his or her good work.** • Make a big, old-fashioned Sunday dinner. Include extended family if they live nearby. • **Play a Bible trivia game as a family.**

FEBRUARY

1 Family Night. Play relaxing music and make Valentines.

2 Invite one of your child's friends over to play.

3 Make your husband's favorite food for dinner.

4 Pile into bed as a family and read aloud.

5 Treat your children to a special snack at the grocery store.

6 Organize a "field trip" for the neighborhood to an indoor playground.

7 Fill a box with craft items to use on a rainy day.

8 Paint handprints to frame for daddy and grandparents. These would make great Valentine's Day surprises.

9 Family Night. Go for a drive and have the family play 20 Questions to guess the destination.

10 Teach your child an age-appropriate chore, very patiently.

11 Practice cutting out hearts; decorate your home for Valentine's Day.

12 Get a sitter and go out on a date with your husband.

13 Write a love letter to your husband.

14 Valentine's Day. Celebrate with a tea party for your little ones.

15 Share Christ with a neighbor.

16 Call someone who lives alone, to chat.

17 Family Night. Take turns sharing what you like about each family member.

18 Have a "Welcome Home, Daddy" party. Hang balloons and streamers, fix his favorite dinner, and then give him an hour to himself.

19 Update your prayer journal.

20 Invite a neighbor and her children to go along on an errand. Conclude with lunch out.

21 Let your children fingerpaint with pudding. Clean-up is delicious!

22 Make a fort inside with blankets.

23 Spend a quiet evening with your husband without the television.

24 Make a cup of tea, get out the garden catalogs, and plan ahead for spring planting. Take time to relax and imagine you're smelling the flowers!

25 In honor of Jesus' birthday, do something kind for someone. An idea: Call or write your mother-in-law to thank her for her son.

26 Family Night. Watch home movies or look at photos of when mom and dad were kids.

27 Plan out your family celebrations for March. Remember to include a Date Night, weekly Family Nights, anniversaries, birthdays, other special occasions, and opportunities to serve others in the name of Jesus.

28 Make today Praise Day. Give glory to God for your family, your home, your world.

29 Have a Leap Day party. Play leapfrog.

Sunday Specials
- After church, go to lunch at a family-style restaurant with a buffet. Don't forget to say a blessing! • **This is the day of rest. Spend time as a family reading the Bible and then take a family nap or have quiet time.** • Invite an elderly friend to attend church with you. • **Do a good deed as a family.**

MARCH

1 Go to the library; look for books on recycling and by Dr. Seuss!

2 Dr. Seuss' birthday. Read *Green Eggs and Ham* as a family and serve eggs with spinach or green food coloring at breakfast.

3 Begin making Easter cards for family members. Share the Easter story as you work.

4 Organize a babysitting co-op with your neighbors and friends.

5 Family Night. Serve spaghetti with plastic gloves instead of forks. Dig right in!

6 Make easy, sweet and crispy treats with cereal and marshmallows.

7 Make a commitment to pray daily for your husband. Ask God to bless him at work and at home.

8 Have an Errand Day. Intersperse "must-do's" with "fun-to-do's," such as lunch out or a trip to the library.

9 Play restaurant. Make a menu and cook dinner; let the kids pretend to take your order and serve.

10 Sort through the kids' clothes looking for items they've outgrown.

11 Farm out the kids and have a special dinner at home with your husband.

12 Make the Easter Story in Eggs — after your children are asleep, so it will be a surprise.

13 Family Night. Have a popcorn and movie night.

14 Make a St. Patrick's Day mobile.

15 Sort through old magazines. Share them with a friend or take them to a retirement center.

16 Give a job to each family member, and begin spring cleaning!

17 St. Patrick's Day. Put a pot of gold (chocolate kisses in gold foil) by each child's bed.

18 Spend the afternoon at a museum.

19 Family Night. Have a Praise Night.

20 Celebrate Spring! Plant flowers inside; picnic in the living room.

21 Take the family and go fly a kite.

22 Make a list of the top ten reasons you love your spouse. Share it with him.

23 Take a minute to encourage another homemaker.

24 Visit the playground and invite a friend.

25 Do something kind in Jesus' name. Reach out to a new neighbor; drop by with cookies or a loaf of banana bread.

26 List the Spring things you're grateful for. Praise God for them.

27 Draw pictures of springtime things. Punch holes through the paper, string yarn through and make a book.

28 Family Night. Let the kids pick the event.

29 Plan your April family celebrations.

30 Have a "Welcome Home, Daddy" party this evening.

31 Make a double batch of tonight's dinner and freeze half for later.

Sunday Specials
• Challenge each family member to teach the others a favorite Bible verse. • **Praise God for the love your family shares.** • Invite another family to church with you and have them over for lunch afterward. • **Make a point of meeting someone new at church.**

APRIL

1 Play a joke for April Fool's Day. Serve dinner for breakfast and breakfast for dinner.

2 Family Night. Let your husband choose the activity.

3 While your husband is at work, "steal" his car and clean it inside and out. Leave a love note for him.

4 Serve a family dinner by candlelight.

5 Color springtime pictures and mail them to the grandparents.

6 Visit a pet store. Make up names for the animals.

7 Have a "scavenger hunt" at the grocery store involving items needed for a special meal.

8 Leave your husband a note on the dashboard of his car.

9 Do something nice for a neighbor.

10 Compose a list of 100 reasons why you love your husband. Have it framed.

11 Family Night. Make up a family prayer.

12 Write letters to your children about why you love them. Save the letters until the kids are older.

13 Clip funny comics to pack in your kids' lunches and send to your husband at work.

14 Begin a read-aloud tradition. Read to your family at breakfast.

15 Post Bible verses on the bathroom mirrors and the refrigerator.

16 Family Night. Make music together (even if only with kazoos and rhythm sticks).

17 Offer to take an elderly neighbor shopping. Include your children in the outing.

18 Leave your children with friends for a sleepover and go on a date with your husband. Arrange to return the favor.

19 Spring Cleaning! Clean out a few closets. Let the kids dress up in the old clothes.

20 Take the day off from housework! Spend the day at the park.

21 Prepare for Daddy Day — make cards, cookies, etc.

22 Visit Daddy at work and show him how special he is with cards and treats.

23 Sit outside and blow bubbles!

24 Meet a friend and her children at the park for a picnic.

25 Find a way to compliment the most frustrating person in your life, or do another kind deed, in Jesus' name.

26 Family Night. Make pizza together and give each other backrubs.

27 Plan celebrations for May, and line up your supplies now.

28 Plant flowers with your children. Explain how plants need sunlight and water to grow.

29 Have a car wash day with the kids, and let everyone get wet and soapy (including you).

30 Make small baskets of flowers and decorate a Maypole for May Day, May 1.

Sunday Specials
• Serve lunch at a shelter as a family. • Literally count your blessings together. See which family member can make the longest list! • Have a quiet day. With no telephone, television, or radio to distract you, read the Bible together. • Go to the zoo as a family and praise God for His creation.

MAY

1 May Day. Fill baskets with fresh flowers and treats; hang on friends' and family's doorknobs.

2 Make plans to mark the National Day of Prayer, which is celebrated the first Thursday in May.

3 Make gifts and cards with the kids for their grandmas for Mother's Day.

4 Go bike riding in honor of National Bike Month.

5 Cook a meal with hubby and eat by candlelight.

6 Family Game Night. Serve dinner around a Monopoly board and play for (with?) your food.

7 Visit a local farm and see the new babies. (Call your local 4-H Club.)

8 Mom's Night Out! Go to dinner with a friend and really talk.

9 Learn about a country with your children. Pray for its people and government.

10 If your children don't know it, teach them the Pledge of Allegiance.

11 Make jewelry with string and uncooked pasta. Have a fashion show.

12 Take the kids to lunch at a place with a play area.

13 Ask your husband to say a devotional with you.

14 Family Night. Exercise together.

15 Call your mother and tell her how much you love her.

16 Nab your husband's calendar and add a few "appointments" he can look forward to.

17 Work in the back yard with the kids, then relax in the sun.

18 List summer activities on slips of paper and put them in a jar. Let your child pick one.

19 Update your prayer journal.

20 Pack a picnic and surprise Daddy at work.

21 Plant sunflowers.

22 Family "camp-out," inside or out. Cook hot dogs; sing songs.

23 Plan your meals for all of June. Two hours now will save time and hassle then.

24 Date Night. Go to the movie *he* really wants to see (or rent the video).

25 Christmas in May. Greet the mail carrier with lemonade and cookies.

26 Invent three new games for the wading pool. Get Daddy involved after work.

27 Proclaim Dad King for a Day this Saturday. Let him watch sports without interruption, and have the kids do something special for him.

28 Get up early today and spend some quality time with God. Ask Him to show you the areas in your life that need work.

29 Family fingerpainting night. (Outside!)

30 Plan your special days for June. Don't forget Father's Day, family nights, mom's private time!

31 Celebrate the end of May. Bake a cake and make lemonade.

Sunday Specials
• Get up early and cook a super breakfast. Thank God for your family as you serve them. • **On Mother's Day, thank God for your mother. Reflect on the day you became a mother yourself.** • Spend a quiet afternoon at home, resting and thanking the Lord for his goodness. • **Spend time in prayer together for your marriage.**

JUNE

1 Rise early and pray for your husband. Commit to making June a special month for him.

2 Tape the family singing songs. Mail copies to the grandparents.

3 Family Night. Organize a family game of baseball. Include the neighbors.

4 Bake with the kids and don't say a word about the mess. Cookies, anyone?

5 Spend time with the kids planning a special Father's Day party.

6 Go to the library and list 15 to 20 books your family would like to read. Check out a few each week.

7 Give your husband a coupon for an entire day to himself, either at home or away.

8 Create a zoo with sidewalk chalk. Think of zoo animals and draw, draw, draw.

9 Celebrate your pet's birthday. If you don't know when it is, today's good.

10 Organize a summer play group.

11 Write a love note on the toilet paper for your husband.

12 Family Night. Put a flagpole on the house in preparation for Flag Day.

13 Write to a long-lost friend. Send family photos and your kids' drawings of themselves.

14 Flag Day. Make a flag or color a picture of a flag.

15 Run a bath for your husband. Wash his hair by candlelight and play soft music.

16 Go for a family bike ride.

17 Interview your grandmother or mother about life when she was growing up.

18 Hug Day. Try to get a hug every hour from each person.

19 Family Night. Serve a picnic supper, complete with gummy worms. Tease the kids and pretend the worms are real.

20 Remember to pray daily for your husband and children.

21 Celebrate summer. Crank up some homemade ice cream.

22 Buy a book on marriage.

23 Go downtown and look at tall buildings. Make buildings out of boxes.

24 Date Night. Pull out those old love letters and get mushy!

25 Do something kind in Jesus' name.

26 Family Night. Serve a dippin' dinner — chicken with barbecue sauce, perhaps, with cut-up veggies and ranch dressing, chips and salsa, ladyfingers and pudding, etc. Then take a dip in the wading pool.

27 Visit a farmer's market. Draw fruits and vegetables. Try a new vegetable tonight.

28 Praise Day. Praise God for all of His attributes. Also lift up your husband in prayer.

29 Plan your family celebrations for July.

30 Pull that red wagon on an evening walk and greet your neighbors.

Sunday Specials
• Praise Day! Spend the day praising God, and try not to ask Him for anything all day. • **Father's Day. Make Dad a special breakfast and let him take a nap after church.** • Go out for ice cream after church. • **Color pictures as a family of things you're grateful to God for.**

JULY

1 Pray for your children and their safety. Also pray for the people in their lives, such as babysitters and friends.

2 Practice the Pledge of Allegiance with your little ones.

3 Bake a birthday cake for our country.

4 Decorate the kids' bikes with red, white, and blue streamers. Have a neighborhood parade and finish with a picnic.

5 Sing a hymn to your child a bedtime.

6 Read The Tale of Peter Rabbit in honor of Beatrix Potter's birthday.

7 Teach your kids about the five senses. Practice with foods and items like feathers and sandpaper.

8 Family Night. Make a gigantic ice cream sundae in a huge bowl, and let the whole gang dig in.

9 Re-inspect your home for fire and other safety hazards.

10 Make a double batch of dinner and freeze one to eat later or share with someone in need.

11 Create a centerpiece from things in your own backyard.

12 Praise Day. Praise God for your children, and praise them for things they do well.

13 Family Night. Plan a camping trip for this summer. Invite extended family members.

14 Send a recent photo with a loving note to your kids' grandparents.

15 Pick blueberries with your children, and make cobbler. Freeze some berries for pancakes!

16 Serve your husband coffee as he is getting ready for work.

17 Learn about a state; make a meal that's a specialty of that state.

18 Make a coupon jar for the money you save using coupons; let the money add up for a special purchase.

19 Drive to a surprise destination, and give the kids clues as you go.

20 Commemorate the first moon landing, which took place in 1969.

21 Family Night. Let the kids pick the menu and activity.

22 Make a trip to an indoor play space. Invite a friend.

23 Beat the heat; stay inside and work a puzzle together.

24 Praise Day. Read the Bible aloud.

25 Do an act of kindness in Jesus' name. You could make dinner for a friend who needs a break.

26 Turn on the sprinkler and cool off in the water.

27 Bugs Bunny's birthday. Watch a cartoon and giggle together. Serve carrots at dinner.

28 Knock on a neighbor's door and introduce yourself.

29 Plan your family celebrations for August; gather supplies.

30 Family Night. Grill hamburgers and hot dogs for dinner.

31 Date Night. Drag a blanket outside and look at the stars.

Sunday Specials
• Make a point of being ready for church 15 minutes early. Enjoy the peace as you drive to church. • Take turns sharing what your dream vacation would be over Sunday lunch. • Discuss the concept of tithing with your children. • Have a family snuggle after church.

Holidays & Everydays

AUGUST

1. Bake a cake to celebrate the new month.
2. Family Night. Act out favorite Bible stories.
3. Go out to dinner with a neighbor.
4. Visit a museum. Give Daddy a report at dinner.
5. Make a trip to the library. Get a kids' cookbook and make dinner with the kids.
6. Date Night. Try a new restaurant. Share a gooey dessert!
7. Recruit a friend and try once-a-month cooking.
8. Mom's Bath Night. Dad can entertain the kids while you soak with a book.
9. Write to a political official with your views on an important subject.
10. Talk to your children about Jesus. Tell them what He means to you and why you pray to Him.
11. Fill a prescription bottle with notes that say, "one night of fun," "a walk in the park," etc. Give it to your husband with a "note from the doctor."
12. Family Night. Make pizza from scratch and try out some new toppings.
13. Take a nature walk. Use what you find in a centerpiece for the table.
14. Make leaf rubbings with your children. Talk about God's creation.
15. Put a special Bible verse in your husband's briefcase and on your children's pillows.
16. Have a Lazy Day. Eat whatever, whenever, for breakfast; stay in pajamas however long; watch cartoons in the morning; nap; hang out at home. Cap off the day with a Lazy Dinner, such as cereal or pizza.
17. Farm out the kids and have a "special" surprise waiting for hubby when he gets home.
18. Update your prayer journal.
19. Children's Day. Let the child who's headed back to school pick the activity and the menu.
20. Visit a shut-in and give the gift of time.
21. Family Night. Exercise as a family.
22. Help your children set up a lemonade stand. Give away the lemonade!
23. Thank your mother-in-law for giving birth to your husband.
24. Go a day without talking on the phone. Play with the kids instead.
25. Do something kind for someone else in honor of Jesus.
26. Tackle a cleaning project you've been putting off. Invite your child to help.
27. Throw a Daddy's Home party. Decorate, celebrate, then give him an hour to himself.
28. Send a loving note to the shut-in you visited last week. Include pictures from the kids.
29. Prepare for next month's celebrations.
30. Family Night. Create a new game to play as a family.
31. Have a picnic in the back yard.

Sunday Specials
• Spend some time praying for your church. Ask God to protect and strengthen its leaders. • **Take a family drive in the afternoon. Investigate a nearby town or a new park.** • Memorize a special Bible verse and put it to music. • **Pray as a family for all of your friends and loved ones who are sick or lonely.**

SEPTEMBER

1 Celebrate the first day of September. Buy a big new box of crayons and color your world (on paper, of course).

2 Go on an outing to feed the birds or visit a park.

3 Start a compost pile. Teach your children to conserve what God has given us.

4 Decorate special cards for the grandparents and send them off!

5 Family Night. Shoot some hoops together.

6 Have a neighborhood clean-up day.

7 Art Day. Learn about a painter and get out the easels.

8 Take a roll of black-and-white film of the kids. It will last longer than color.

9 Eat your way through the ABC's. Find a food for each letter, and teach the alphabet while you eat.

10 Date Night. It's your husband's turn to plan a low-cost night out.

11 Teach your children to sort clothes by color and fabric weight.

12 Family Night. Play "Remember When?" Share memories of favorite together times.

13 Put a lipstick kiss on a small piece of paper and slip it into your husband's pocket.

14 Dig up your old typewriter and let the kids practice typing.

15 Encourage a mom who works outside the home with a phone call, card, or meal.

16 Spontaneous Day. Don't plan anything, and see what develops.

17 Dad's Night Out. Invite your husband to call a friend and go to dinner or a sporting event.

18 Family Night. Study your family tree with your children. Share memories of your relatives.

19 Let your kids be "Mom for a Day" and see how they perceive your role.

20 Call a long-distance friend or relative and catch up. Don't look at the clock; really focus on your conversation.

21 Go for a walk and look for early signs of fall. Thank God for His seasons.

22 Have a "Goodbye to Summer" party with the neighborhood stay-at-home moms and kids.

23 Make an apple pie from scratch to celebrate fall.

24 Update your prayer journal.

25 Do something kind for your child's teacher or someone else in Jesus' name.

26 Family Night. Go out for ice cream.

27 Schedule a marriage conference for your husband and you.

28 Take some time to plan for next month's family activities and celebrations. Look ahead to the holiday season and prayerfully set your priorities.

29 Mom's Night Out. You deserve it! Will you call a friend to join you or enjoy some time alone?

30 Rake leaves for an elderly person.

Sunday Specials
• Read a Christian children's story as a family. Talk about it. • **Celebrate Grandparents' Day**, the first Sunday after Labor Day. Show your grandparents (and your children's) how much they are loved. • Write a journal entry about your day. Thank God for all of your blessings. • **Learn a new Bible verse as a family.**

OCTOBER

1 Organize a trip to a farm and hayride for neighborhood stay-at-home parents and kids.

2 Ask your child to draw a picture for your family Christmas card. Take it to a copy shop and have it printed in red or green ink. Begin addressing envelopes now!

3 Family Night. Find an uplifting story in the newspaper and share it.

4 Have a family fire drill. Talk about fire safety.

5 Take stock of your Christmas shopping lists. Pray that God will help you keep your focus as the season nears.

6 Have a no-TV, no-video day.

7 After the kids are asleep, spend time really talking with your husband. Ask him how you can be a better wife. Praise him for the ways he is a good husband.

8 Pray for the families of SIDS victims.

9 Visit the library for storytime. Get a book of magic tricks.

10 Learn a magic trick and perform it for the kids. (Don't reveal your secret.)

11 Family Night. Make a scarecrow as a family.

12 Read the comics to the kids. Let them color in the newspaper.

13 Make apple butter or applesauce.

14 Arrange a potluck dinner for next weekend.

15 Visit a shut-in; take some of your apple butter!

16 Have a vegetarian dinner. Try a food you've never served before.

17 Update your prayer journal.

18 Family Night. Go to a pumpkin patch and pick the perfect pumpkin.

19 Make an autumn centerpiece with your children.

20 Carve the pumpkin as a family. Roast the seeds, pop popcorn and drink apple cider.

21 Praise Day! Sing along with a tape or Christian radio station.

22 Take a nature walk to look for leaves and acorns.

23 Get dressed up and go meet Daddy for lunch.

24 Family Night. Organize your family photos and talk about the good times you've shared.

25 Do something kind in Jesus' name.

26 Play touch football with your children and their friends.

27 Take a few minutes to write in your child's journal.

28 Get down on the floor and play joyfully with your children.

29 Plan your November celebrations and activities. Make a point of including some down time.

30 Leaf Day. Spend the day working in the yard. Teach the younger kids to rake leaves.

31 Help your church hold a fall festival.

Sunday Specials
• Take a drive after church and admire the colorful leaves. • **After the children are asleep, spend an hour in prayer with your husband.** • Read from the NIV Bible, first published in October 1978. • **Take some time to visit the sick and elderly in your church.**

NOVEMBER

1 Celebrate All Saints' Day with your family.

2 Decorate your home for Thanksgiving.

3 Set your deadline for completion of Christmas shopping for sometime this month.

4 Make a list of things you want to accomplish before the end of the year. Pray over the list.

5 Family Night. Light a fire; stretch out with pillows and blankets, and tell funny stories.

6 Have a play day with your children. Let them choose the games and toys.

7 Errand Day. Plan something fun for your kids to enjoy (lunch out?) amid the shopping.

8 Bring breakfast to your husband in bed.

9 Spend an evening with the catalogs and finish your Christmas shopping early.

10 Grab a friend and do your once-a-month cooking. You'll enjoy the holiday festivities more if you're not worrying about the evening meal.

11 Invite someone who lives alone to join you for Thanksgiving.

12 Color Thanksgiving pictures with the kids and mail them to the grandparents.

13 Family Night. Play board games; serve hot chocolate and popcorn.

14 Exercise with the kids. Really exhaust yourselves!

15 Errand Day. Give your children money and help them buy Christmas presents for Daddy.

16 Make a meal with the children; take it to a sick or elderly neighbor.

17 Take your kids and a friend to an indoor play place.

18 Date Night. Give your husband a slow, luxurious massage.

19 Put a wholesome family movie on the television and take a break. Turn off the telephone ringer, pop popcorn, and unwind!

20 Update your prayer journal.

21 Family Night. Assemble food baskets for the needy.

22 Mom's Night In. Take a long, hot bath and de-stress.

23 Set up a corner in the kitchen with pots and pans and macaroni so the little ones can help you "cook."

24 Write an entry in each child's journal about thankfulness.

25 Take this opportunity to be kind to a challenging relative in Jesus' name.

26 Praise Day. Praise God for His bounteous creation.

27 Decorate an outside tree for Christmas.

28 Take a deep breath and organize your December calendar. Distinguish what is required and what is extra.

29 Choose a needy family to sponsor for Christmas. Get their wish list from your church or a social service agency.

30 Family Night. Make cookies together.

Sunday Specials

• Take a long walk as a family after church. • Go through closets and drawers to find unused coats and other clothing you can donate to a shelter. Deliver the items as a family. • Put all hands to work in the kitchen taking care of do-ahead projects for Thanksgiving dinner. • **Praise God together for your many blessings.**

DECEMBER

1 Write your husband a love letter.

2 Have an inside day. Work on homemade Christmas gifts with the children.

3 Date Night. Take time to really talk, whether at home or out together.

4 Family Night. Write the family Christmas letter.

5 Put on some festive music and finish addressing Christmas cards.

6 Dad's Shopping Night. Drop a few hints and give your husband the night away from home.

7 Clean-Up Day. Tackle a few chores that have been piling up.

8 Invite a friend and her children over to bake cookies.

9 Go to the library and check out some good books about the real Christmas story. Have your own story hour at home.

10 Help your children pick out some of their toys to give away. Drive together to the agency who will receive them.

11 Update your prayer journal.

12 Family Night. Take a Christmas family photo, at home or in a studio.

13 Slip a sweet note into your husband's pocket or briefcase.

14 Spend time with the Lord. Give your lists to Him and let Him set your priorities.

15 Take your children to sing carols at a nursing home.

16 Invite some friends over to pray in the New Year.

17 Bake cookies for the mail carrier and trash collector.

18 Teach your children a Christmas song they haven't heard before.

19 Praise Day. Praise God for the gift of His Son.

20 Family Night. Read the Christmas story from the Bible.

21 Snuggle with your hubby and gaze at the Christmas tree.

22 Color in a coloring book with your children. It's therapeutic!

23 Go for a drive as a family and admire the Christmas lights.

24 Deliver packages to your Christmas family.

25 Christmas Day. Celebrate Jesus' birthday.

26 Ask your husband to keep the kids, and take advantage of the after-Christmas sales.

27 Make notes about this year's Christmas celebration in your child's journal or your holiday scrapbook.

28 Help your children write notes to thank their relatives and friends for Christmas gifts.

29 Do something for exercise, whether a walk outdoors or an indoor workout.

30 Fill in next year's calendar with birthdays, anniversaries, and other special occasions.

31 Pray in the New Year (see page 93).

Sunday Specials
• Pick out the family Christmas tree together. • **Decorate your home for Christmas. Don't forget the mistletoe!** • Bake something special for your adopted Christmas family together. • **Have a quiet day. After church, relax in front of the fire or take a nap.**

Recommended Reading

These books and other resources have been recommended in the pages of *The Proverbs 31 Homemaker* newsletter, and are categorized here for your reference.

Children's Devotions

• For toddlers:

First Steps by Paul Loth

God Is With Me by Debby Anderson

God Made All the Colors by Linden Evans

Growing God's Way to See and Share by V. Gilbert Beers

High Chair Devotions by Marilyn J. Woody

I Go To Church by Marian Bennet

Read-Aloud Bible Stories (two volumes) by Ella Lindvall

The Toddlers Bible by V. Gilbert Beers

The Toddlers Bedtime Story Book by V. Gilbert Beers

• For older pre-schoolers and school-age children:

The Bible in Pictures for Little Eyes by Kenneth Taylor

The Boy Who Gave His Lunch Away by Dave Hill

Egermeier's Bible Story Book by Elsie Egermeier, revised by Arlene Hall

I Can Talk to God Anytime, Anyplace by Jennie Davis

Little Visits® series by Mary Manz Simon

Sometimes I Get Lonely: Psalm 42 for Children, one of the 15 "David and I" titles by Elspeth Campbell Murphy

Theirs Is the Kingdom by Lowell Haan

Walking With Jesus by V. Gilbert Beers

Who Is Jesus? by Carolyn Nystrom

Christian Fiction

The Girl From Montana, The Story of a Whim, Aunt Crete's Emancipation, and other novels by Grace Livingston Hill

Piercing the Darkness, The Prophet, This Present Darkness, and other titles by Frank Peretti

Home Management/Finances

Catch up in the Kitchen by the Sidetracked Home Executive Sisters

Dinner's in the Freezer! More Mary and Less Martha by Jill Bond (available from Great Christian Books, 1-800-775-5422; also ask for *Jill's Favorite Freezer Tips*, which is free). For more information on Jill Bond's upcoming book, *Writing to God's Glory*, or her audio and video tapes, contact The Bonding Place, P.O. Box 736, Lake Hamilton, FL 33851, 407-453-0663, ext. 2.

Financial Planning for Couples by Adrian Berg

Miserly Moms Living on One Income in a Two-Income Economy by Jonni Stivers McCoy (contact Miserly Moms, P.O. Box 32174, San Jose, CA 95152-2174)

Recommended Reading

More Hours in My Day by Emilie Barnes (for more info, send SASE to More Hours in My Day, 2838 Rumsey Dr., Riverside, CA 92506)

Once-a-Month Cooking by Mimi Wilson and Mary Beth Lagerborg

Weekend Decorating by Leslie Linsley

Working from Home by Lindsey O'Connor

Marriage

52 Dates for You and Your Mate by Dave and Claudia Arp

Hidden Keys of a Loving, Lasting Relationship by Gary Smalley (contains *If Only He Knew* and *For Better or For Best*)

The Hidden Value of a Man by Gary Smalley and John Trent, Ph.D

How to Have a Happy Marriage by Dave and Vera Mace

Letters to Karen by Charlie Shedd

Sex Begins in the Kitchen by Kevin Leman

Parenting/Family

Growing Kids God's Way by Gary and Anne Marie Ezzo

Home Grown Kids by Raymond and Dorothy Moore

Let's Make a Memory by Gloria Gaither and Shirley Dobson

Mastering Motherhood by Barbara Bush

A Mother's Manual for Holiday Survival by Kathy Peel and Judie Byrd

A Mother's Manual for Summer Survival by Kathy Peel and Joy Mahaffey

Positive Discipline by Jane Nelsen

The Stomach Virus and Other Forms of Family Bonding by Kathy Peel

Victorian Family Celebrations by Sarah Ban Breathnach

When Can a Child Believe? by Eugene Chamberlain

When You Feel Like Screaming! Help for Frustrated Mothers by Pat Hobb and Grace Ketterman, M.D.

Prayer

I'm Having a Baby — Help Me, Lord! by Cathy Hickling

In Everything By Prayer prayer journal by Sandy Day ($16.50 from Caleb Ministries, Inc., P.O. Box 470093, Charlotte, N.C. 28247; 704-846-5372)

What Happens When Women Pray by Evelyn Christenson

Women

All in Good Time by Donna Otto

Being a Wild, Wonderful Woman for God by Becky Tirabassi

Between Women of God: The Gentle Art of Mentoring by Donna Otto

In the Company of Women by Dr. Brenda Hunter

Mentors for Mothers (24-week group study program available from Donna Otto, 11453 N. 53rd Place, Scottsdale, AZ 85254)

The Proverbs 31 Lady and Other Impossible Dreams by Marsha Drake

The Stay-at-Home Mom by Donna Otto

Survival for Busy Women by Emilie Barnes

About our Authors

This index offers information about each person who contributed to *The Best of The Proverbs 31 Homemaker* and tells you where his or her work can be found.

Christine Anderson lives in Huntersville, N.C., with her husband, Peter, and their four children: Ashley, born in 1980; Markham, born in 1982; Eric, born in 1983; and Caitlyn, born in 1987. Before becoming a mom, Christine worked as a registered nurse. She enjoys reading, baking, walking, and studying symbolism in the Scriptures. She is active in a local Christian Mothers' Group, and her "Quiet-Time Testimony" (page 16) was excerpted from a presentation she made to the group.

Meg Avey recently moved to Louisville, Ky., from Pennsylvania with her husband, Scott, and their son Steven, born in 1990. She is a childbirth educator and a homeschooling mom. She enjoys puppet ministry, gardening, skiing, and tennis. Meg has written several regular columns for the newsletter. She contributed to the book "The Traveling Man" (page 24), "The Overscheduled Family" (page 46), "Accidents Happen" (page 49), and "Every Day is Valentine's Day" (page 85).

Carol L. Baldwin lives in Charlotte, N.C., with her husband, Creighton, and four daughters. (Their oldest, Leslie, attends King College in Bristol, Tennessee.) Lindsey (born in 1979), Lisa (1988), Lori (1989), and Lydia (1991) keep Carol busy with their activities. She enjoys writing and playing tennis in her "free" time; she has written for several national publications and provided some devotionals for the *Women's Devotional Bible* (Zondervan, 1990). Carol wrote "Mothers Matter" (page 33) because, as daughter Lisa said, "The world would be a different place without mothers."

Meredith Banks lives in Charlotte, N.C., with her husband, Christopher. She studied English literature in college and enjoys writing. In "The Hardest Part of Marriage" (page 26), she urges wives to yield to the Holy Spirit and, by doing so, to experience the blessings the Lord has in store for their families. Meredith also contributed to "Cost-Conscious Decorating Ideas" (page 84).

Cheryl Bessett lives in Wheat Ridge, Colo., with her husband, Darren, and their two children, Hannah and Daelin. Cheryl went to college intending to make law her career; while there, she met her husband and earned a bachelor's degree in Speech. Upon the conception of their first child, Cheryl chose to remain at home and aspire to a career as a full-time wife and mother. She wrote "Helping Each Other" (page 62) the second Christmas after Hannah was born.

Jeannie Marendt DeSena lives in Charlotte, N.C., with her supportive husband, Curtis, and their daughter, Olivia Marie, who was born in August 1994. Jeannie has a background in newspaper journalism; she has worked as a writer, editor, and page designer, and she taught communications labs at University of Florida while earning a master's degree in mass communication with a supporting field in children's literature. Jeannie enjoys playing the piano, collecting children's books, taking pictures of Olivia, keeping a journal, and hiking in the Blue Ridge Mountains with her family. The editor and designer of this book, she also contributed "The Perfect Day" (page 42).

Sidney Lefevers Dunlap lives in Raleigh, N.C., with her husband, Hughes, and their children: Davis, born in 1979; Hannah, born in 1981; Jake, born in in 1987; and Sam, born in 1989. Sidney works as a substitute teacher and as the billing secretary for her husband's commercial landscape business. She is active in her church's Christian education, youth, and evangelism ministries. Her work has appeared in a magazine for Christian educators. Sidney is seeking a master's degree in education. She and her sister, Susan Yount, are authors of "Hatching the Easter Story" (page 89).

Susan Gardner and her husband, Mike, are the parents of Elizabeth, born in 1981, and John, born in 1983. Susan teaches ladies' Bible studies at her church in Charlotte, N.C., and helps Mike with the family business, Elizabeth's Shoes. Her hobbies include playing the piano and singing. Susan wrote "Train Up a Child" (page 38).

Susan Godley lives in Charlotte, N.C., with her husband, Rod, and their children, Jason, born in 1992, and Luke, born in 1994. They were awaiting the birth of their third child as the book went to press. Susan is the accountant for *The Proverbs 31 Homemaker* newsletter, and she enjoys sewing and walking. She wrote a "Quiet-Time Testimony" (page 17) "to remind women that their personal relationship with God through quiet time is their first priority."

Shirley Gray and her husband, Tony, are parents of twins Colin and Preston, born in 1990, and Maggie, born in 1993. They live in Matthews, N.C. Before staying at home with her children, Shirley was a physical therapy assistant. She now works from home decorating cakes. Shirley wrote "Building a Household" (page 51) and "A Homemaker's Prayer" (page 14).

Rhonda Brownlee Jaynes lives in Charlotte, N.C., with her husband, Melvin. She and her mother are partners in a residential cleaning business; Rhonda discovered the newsletter at a client's home. "Even though I'm not a mom, I highly support 'at-home' moms and their values," she writes. Rhonda makes crafts to sell and also is beginning an interior design business. She contributed "Down-to-Earth Decorating" (page 82).

Carol Mader and her husband, Ralph, live in Huntsville, Ala., with their sons Ivan, born in 1990, and Hans, born in 1992. She homeschools the boys, writes for a parenting newspaper, and has "many children's books waiting for a publisher." The newsletter's biblical point of view appeals to Carol. She wrote "A Poem for My Husband" (page 25).

Jennifer McHugh and her husband, Mike, are the parents of Morgan, born in 1990, Mary Madison, born in 1994, and Jake, born in 1995. Jennifer founded *The Proverbs 31 Homemaker* newsletter after moving to Charlotte, N.C., as a wife and mother of one. She jokes that she has "no life" outside her family and the ministry! She enjoys listening to contemporary Christian music and, in her rare spare moments, reading Christian fiction. Jennifer wrote many of the selections in this book; they appear on pages 15, 18, 19, 21, 23, 44, 55, 56, 67, 87, and 91. More information about Jennifer and the ministry is found in "From the Editor" (page 8).

Beth McKnight has a background in business and spent six years in commercial real-estate finance before turning her attention to the care of her husband, Brent, and their sons, Brent, born in 1994, and Matthew, born in 1995. They live in Charlotte, N.C. Her hobbies include singing, making crafts, and reading. She contributed "A New Year's Tradition" (page 93).

Sue Rudolph is the mother of ministry founder Jennifer McHugh and a son, Norman Chambers. Sue and her husband, Bob, live in Raleigh, N.C., where she says "keeping the house clean is at least a part-time job." She has been an elementary school teacher for 23 years, and she enjoys playing bridge, spending time with Jennifer, and decorating. Sue wrote "That First Grandchild" (page 59).

Nancee Burnett Skipper and her husband, Dickson, are the proud parents of four boys and two girls: Aaron (born in 1980); Molly (1982); Micah (1983); twins Joshua and Caleb (1986); and Katie (1992). A former fifth-grade schoolteacher, Nancee is an active homeschool mom and co-leader in the Charlotte area's M.O.M.S. (Mothers of Many Siblings) support group. She was chosen the 1993 North Carolina Homemaker of the Year by Phyllis Schlafly's Eagle Forum. Nancee delights in speaking and writing on the topic of mothering. In the future, she hopes to *enjoy* camping, hiking, and canoeing with her family (who already do!). Her contributions to the book are "Respecting the Individual" (page 40), "Makin' Memories" (page 53) and "Making Time for Yourself" (page 71).

Janet Steddum has lived in Raleigh, N.C., for the past eleven years. According to her husband, Curt, a salesman for IBM, she married well. They are the parents of Catherine, born in 1987; Christopher, in 1988; and Charlotte, in 1991. Prior to becoming a homemaker, Janet worked for IBM as a systems engineer. Everyone in the Steddum family is studying a musical instrument, and they play together for entertainment. Janet's life verse is 1 Thessalonians 4:11. Janet wrote "Homemaker Blues" (page 45), "It's Not in the Budget" (page 75), "Food for Thought" (page 78), "Winning the Grocery Game" (page 80), and "Eating Out for Less" (page 81).

Lysa TerKeurst became co-owner of *The Proverbs 31 Homemaker* newsletter with the July 1994 issue and is the voice of the radio ministry as well as a conference speaker. She lives in Waxhaw, N.C., with her husband, Art, and daughters, Hope, born in 1994, and Ashley, born in 1995. Outside of the ministry, Lysa enjoys exercising and home decorating. She interviewed Marilyn Quayle (page 68) and wrote "My Hunk of Burning Love" (page 73).

Brent Wainscott and his wife, Barbara, live in Charlotte, N.C., with their daughter, Lindsey Ann, born in 1994. Brent is a pilot with USAir and a financial consultant. He enjoys golfing, running, and woodworking. About his article "I Won't Make My Own Soap!" (page 76), he writes, "I know what a struggle it can be to stay on a budget and be a good steward with what God provides."

Marybeth Whalen is a longtime contributor to *The Proverbs 31 Homemaker* and edited the newsletter from the February 1995 through January 1996 issues. She also proposed the idea for the first Proverbs 31 Conference. She and her husband, Curt, live in Charlotte, N.C., with their children, Jack, born in 1992, and Ashleigh, born in 1994. Marybeth is active in a local Christian Mothers' Group, and she enjoys reading Southern fiction and parenting books, and writing for pleasure. She contributed a "Quiet-Time Testimony" (page 16), "What Should I Do?" (page 36), "The Value of Friendship" (page 64), "Donna Otto: Mentors for Moms" (page 65), "Is it Just the Thought that Counts?" (page 88) and some "Cost-conscious Decorating Ideas" (page 84).

Ruth Ann Wilson and her husband, the Rev. Charles Leonard Wilson, live in Charlotte, N.C. They are the parents of Ruthanna (born in 1969), Rachel (1972), Sarah (1973), Reba (1975), Martha (1978), and Daniel (1980). Ruth Ann jokes that "labor management" over six kids keeps her busy; she also enjoys sewing and crafts. She previously worked as a nurse. She contributed a "Quiet-Time Testimony" (page 17) and the essay "From the Mentor" (page 58).

Kevin Woody is one of the newsletter's most prolific contributors. He and his wife, Michelle, also a contributor, live in Raleigh, N.C., with their daughter, Salem, born in 1990, and twin sons, Caleb and Grant, born in 1991. Kevin sells real estate with Howard Perry & Walston/Better Homes & Gardens and enjoys sports and reading. He wrote "Reasons to Endure" (page 12), "He Won't Go to Church" (page 28), "A Question in Her Eyes" (page 30), and "A Father's Treasure" (page 35).

Michelle Woody enjoys playing the piano, singing, relaxing at the beach, and spending time with friends and family — husband Kevin (see above) and children Salem, Caleb, and Grant. Michelle also sells Mary Kay Cosmetics. She wrote "Punishment or Discipline" (page 47) to help struggling homemakers from dysfunctional families who do not have a healthy foundation for parenting.

Debra Yeatts lives in a turn-of-the-century farmhouse in Charlotte, N.C., with her husband, Rodney, and their two children, Kaitlin, born in 1991, and Christian, born in 1992. Debra is a teacher at a Mother's Morning Out program and enjoys gardening, reading, writing, refurbishing her home, and painting. She says being a mother at home has taught her the importance of living a life of simplicity and the joy of knowing the love of God. She contributed "My Life, God's Garment" (page 11) and the essay that gives its title to Chapter One, "Children of God" (page 20).

Susan Lefevers Yount and her husband, Jim, are the parents of Elizabeth Parker, born in 1987, and they are expecting a child in April 1996. They live in Matthews, N.C., where Susan is active in children's church and social ministry outreach at her church. She enjoys walking and keeping journals about her children. She works from home as a medical practice management consultant and does public relations and marketing. She also produces a Santa letter with a Christian perspective and egg sets that help tell the Easter story "so parents have help focusing the spiritual purpose of Christmas and Easter in a secular world." She and her sister, Sidney Lefevers Dunlap, tell how to create the egg sets in "Hatching the Easter Story" (page 89).

"I Saw You Today" (page 60) was published anonymously when it first appeared in the newsletter, and the essay's author wants to go unnamed still. She explains: "I believe the words of this writing were inspired to me through the Holy Spirit of God and were meant to be a message of encouragement to the readers. To place a name and location to the writing would limit its effectiveness. I can be anyone, anywhere; and, indeed, I am but voicing what many others feel. To the stay-at-home moms, I can say, 'Look around. Many are praying for you.' To the ones, like myself, who are watching, I can say, 'Pray.' "

About the Ministry

THE PROVERBS 31 HOMEMAKER MINISTRY is dedicated to glorifying God by providing encouragement and information to homemakers through our monthly newsletter, radio ministry, conferences, encouragement groups, and, now, this book.

The Proverbs 31 Homemaker Ministry began in 1992 when Jennifer McHugh, a new mom, struggled with the decision to become a homemaker. After she and her husband renewed their commitment to Christ, they knew the correct decision for their small family.

The ministry has published a monthly newsletter since August 1992. Now, the radio ministry also reaches women in more than 82 cities. One-minute radio spots provide information on such topics as seasonal activities for children, creative ways to love your husband, and the importance of putting Christ first in everything.

To further encourage and inform women of all ages and occupations, the ministry offers conferences around the country. Conferences are typically held on Saturdays and last either a half or full day. Hosting a conference involves providing a church facility that can hold a minimum of 300 women and providing a few dedicated volunteers. Possible subject areas include building your relationship with the Lord, setting goals and managing the family finances, creating memorable family celebrations, and leading a healthy life.

Proverbs 31 Encouragement Groups began throughout Charlotte, North Carolina — the ministry's home city — in 1995. These groups of women meet at sponsor churches at least twice a month to share with and support one another, and to study what the Bible says about prayer, marriage, parenting, and other topics of interest. There is a time for open discussion and a time for prayer. Child care is available. In the near future, the ministry will offer guidance for women who want to begin encouragement groups in their areas.

We ask your prayers for the Proverbs 31 Homemaker Ministry, and we pray for the needs of our fellow homemakers each month when we come together to mail the newsletter. May God bless us all in our important work.

Order Form

Name: _____

Street Address: _____

City, State, Zip: _____

Telephone Number: _____

Please send me:

❑ ___ copies of *The Best of The Proverbs 31 Homemaker* at $8.95 each.

❑ A subscription to *The Proverbs 31 Homemaker* newsletter at $15 for twelve monthly issues.

❑ One newsletter subscription for myself at $15 and a second one as a gift for $13.

❑ ___ "Homemaking is a Proud Profession" bumper stickers at $3 each.

❑ A free information kit on the Proverbs 31 Conferences.

Shipping (books only):

❑ Book Rate: $1.60 for the first book and 70 cents for each additional book. Surface shipping may take three to four weeks.

❑ Air Mail: $3.50 per book.

Sales tax:
Please add 6% for books, newsletters, and bumper stickers shipped to North Carolina addresses.

Total for books, newsletter subscriptions, bumper stickers $_____

Shipping $_____

N.C. sales tax (if applicable) $_____

TOTAL ENCLOSED $_____

Please send this completed order form plus check or money order to:

PROVERBS 31 HOMEMAKER PRESS
P.O. BOX 17155-96
CHARLOTTE, NC 28270.

Questions? Call 704-849-2270.

Order today!